Time Together

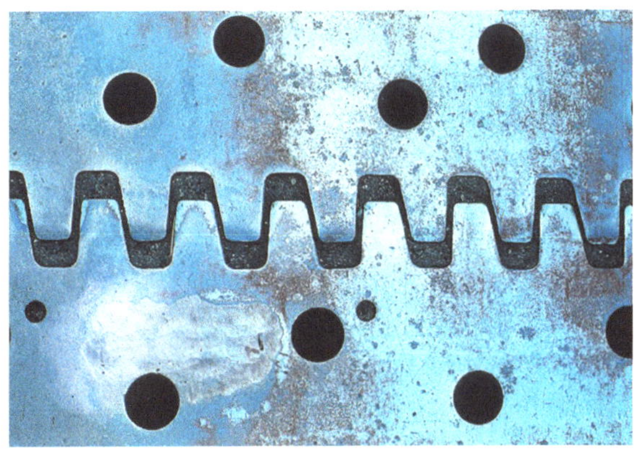

Time Together

poetry by

Naomi Beth Wakan

photography by

Elias Wakan

Shanti Arts Publishing
Brunswick, Maine

TIME TOGETHER

Published by Shanti Arts Publishing
Designed by Shanti Arts Designs

Shanti Arts LLC
193 Hillside Road
Brunswick, Maine 04011
shantiarts.com

Printed in the United States of America

ISBN: 978-1-956056-41-9 (softcover)

Library of Congress Control Number: 2022938029

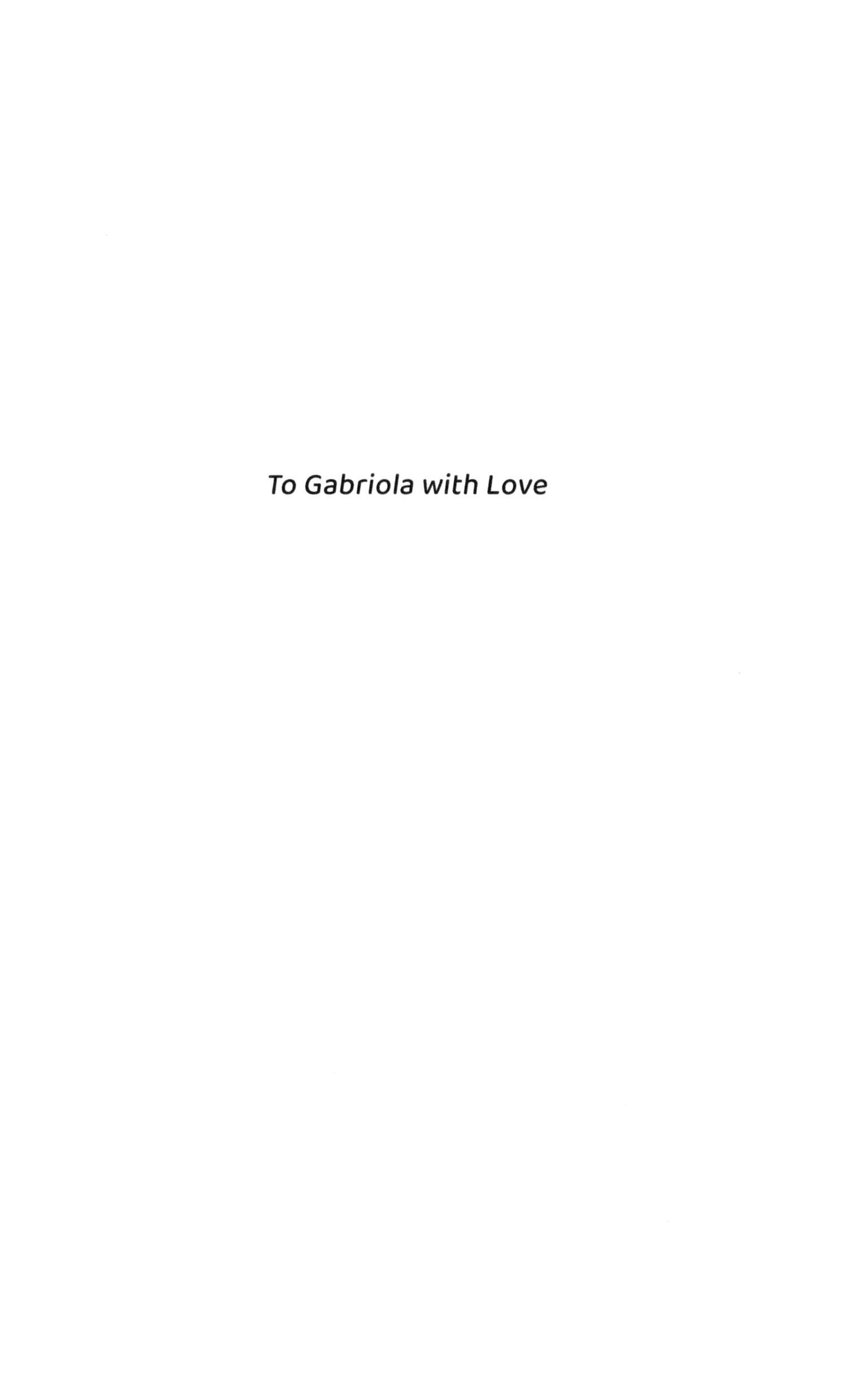

To Gabriola with Love

Contents

Introduction

In our long relationship, of over forty-five years, our roles in respect to each other have changed many times. Sometimes I suggested the adventure and sometimes Eli did. So we wandered and settled and wandered and settled as therapist and carpenter, earth-sheltered house designer and assistant, world travelers, ESL teachers, photo-journalists, publishers, and, finally, landowners on our modest Gabriola half acre with its vinyl-sided cottage, which gave us the base from which to explore our talents in depth—me as a poet and personal essayist, Eli as a sculptor and humming bird guardian. We were able to do this because, at last, we had chosen to live in community, and it was that support that made our creative efforts possible.

—Naomi Beth Wakan

When I first pointed out to Naomi that she had done a few books using other folks' photos to go with her tanka but hadn't done one using mine. I should have known what that would mean. At the moment when I made that casual remark, Naomi was making lunch and was about to put a couple of minutes into her daily crossword while awaiting the food to finish cooking. She responded with what seemed to me to be an odd reply: "Lunch will take a wee bit longer." The reason for the extra time soon became clear, for when lunch was actually served, she had almost finished laying out the guts for this book, *Time Together*, a book that would apparently be using my photos and her poetry. That's it! The story of our long life together. Naomi is fast and I am slow. It is, for us, a successful combination.

—Elias Wakan

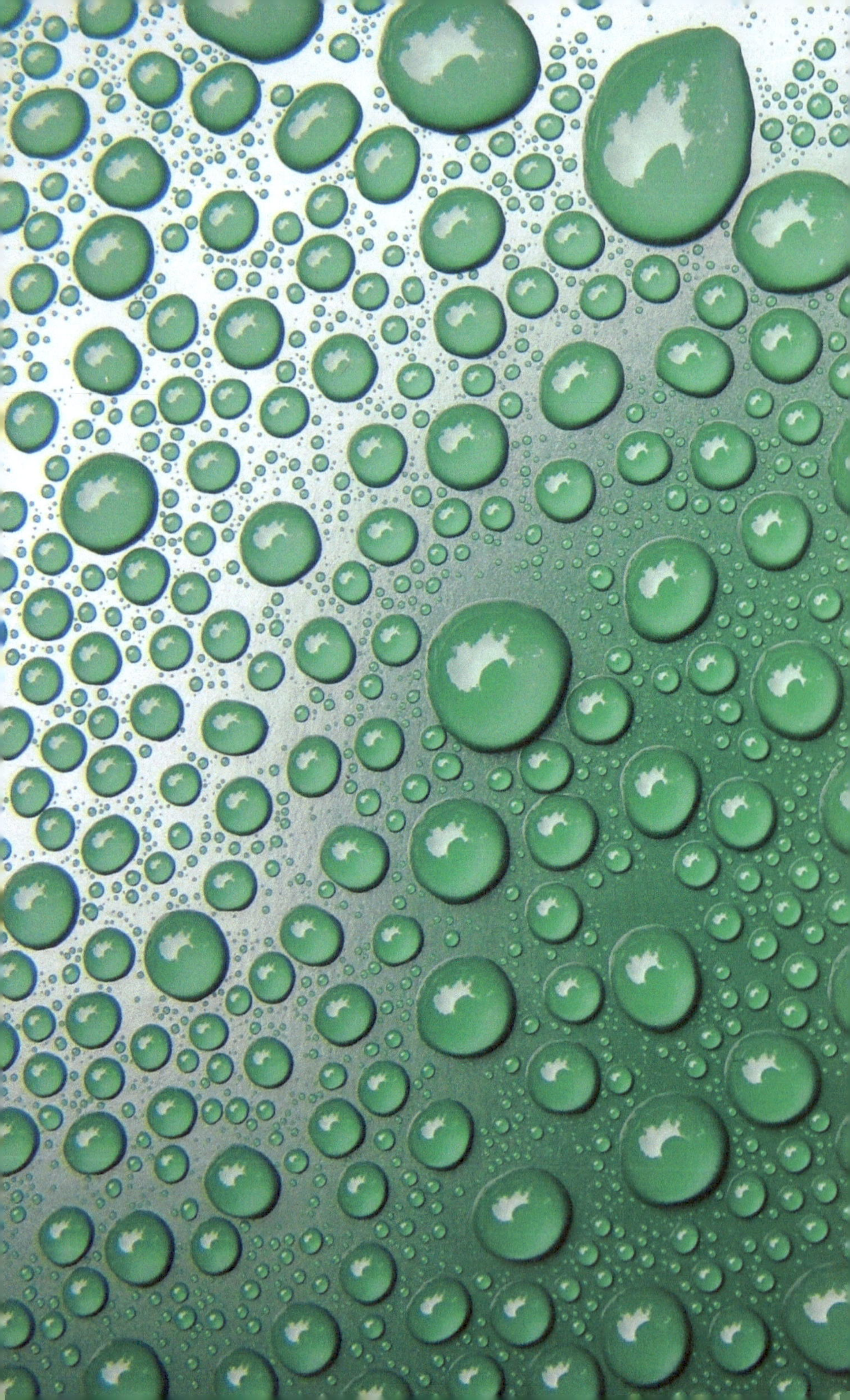

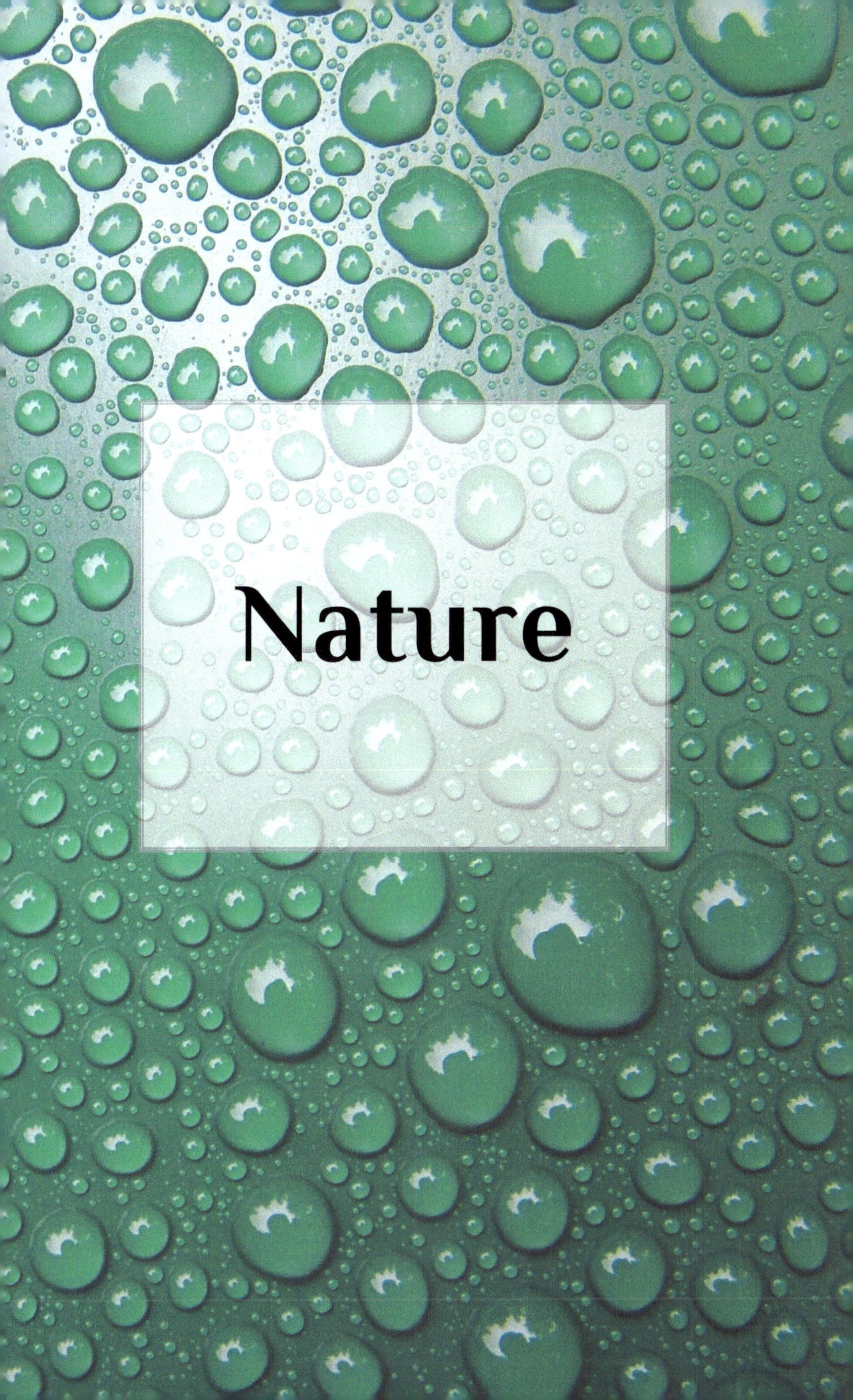
Nature

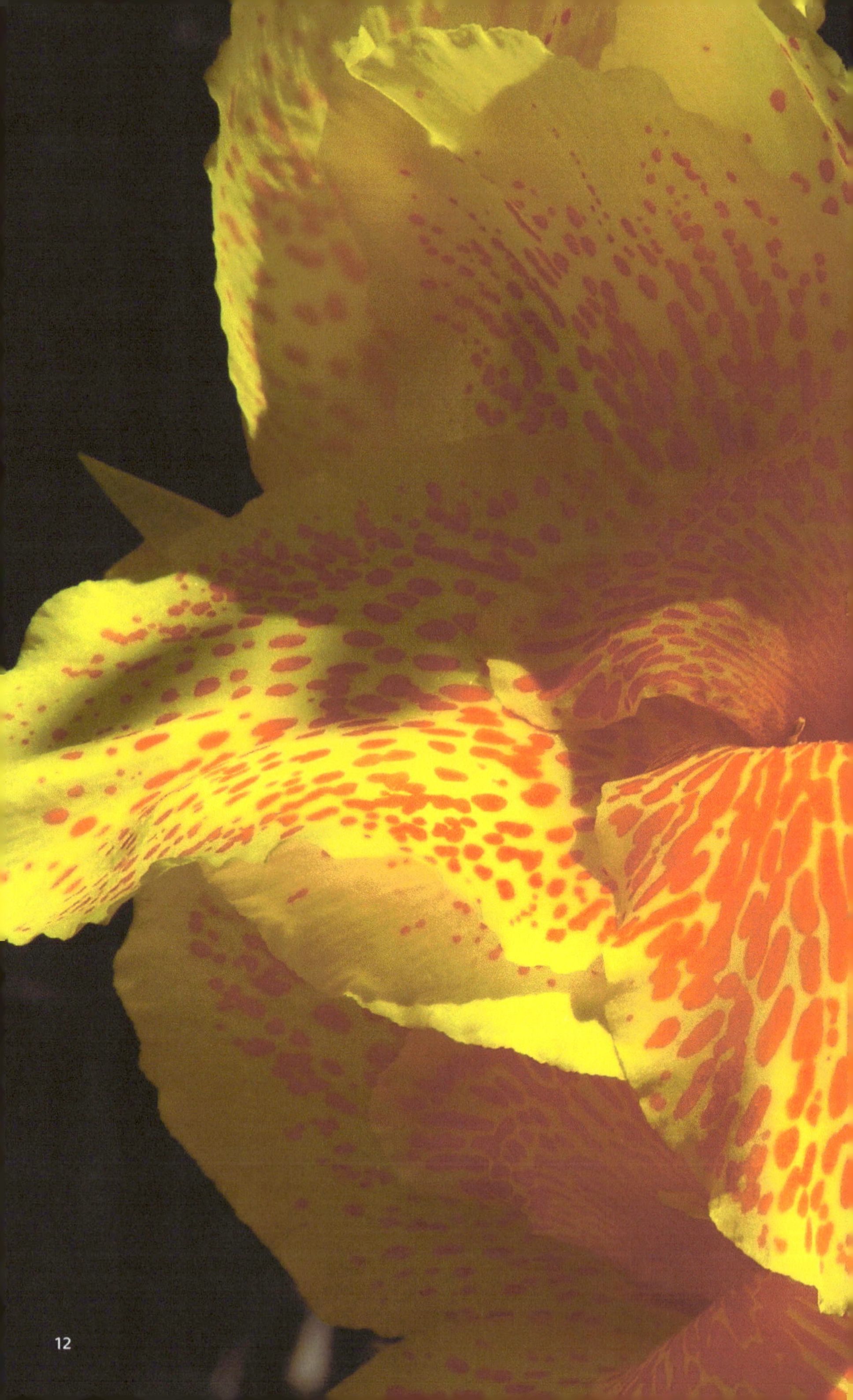

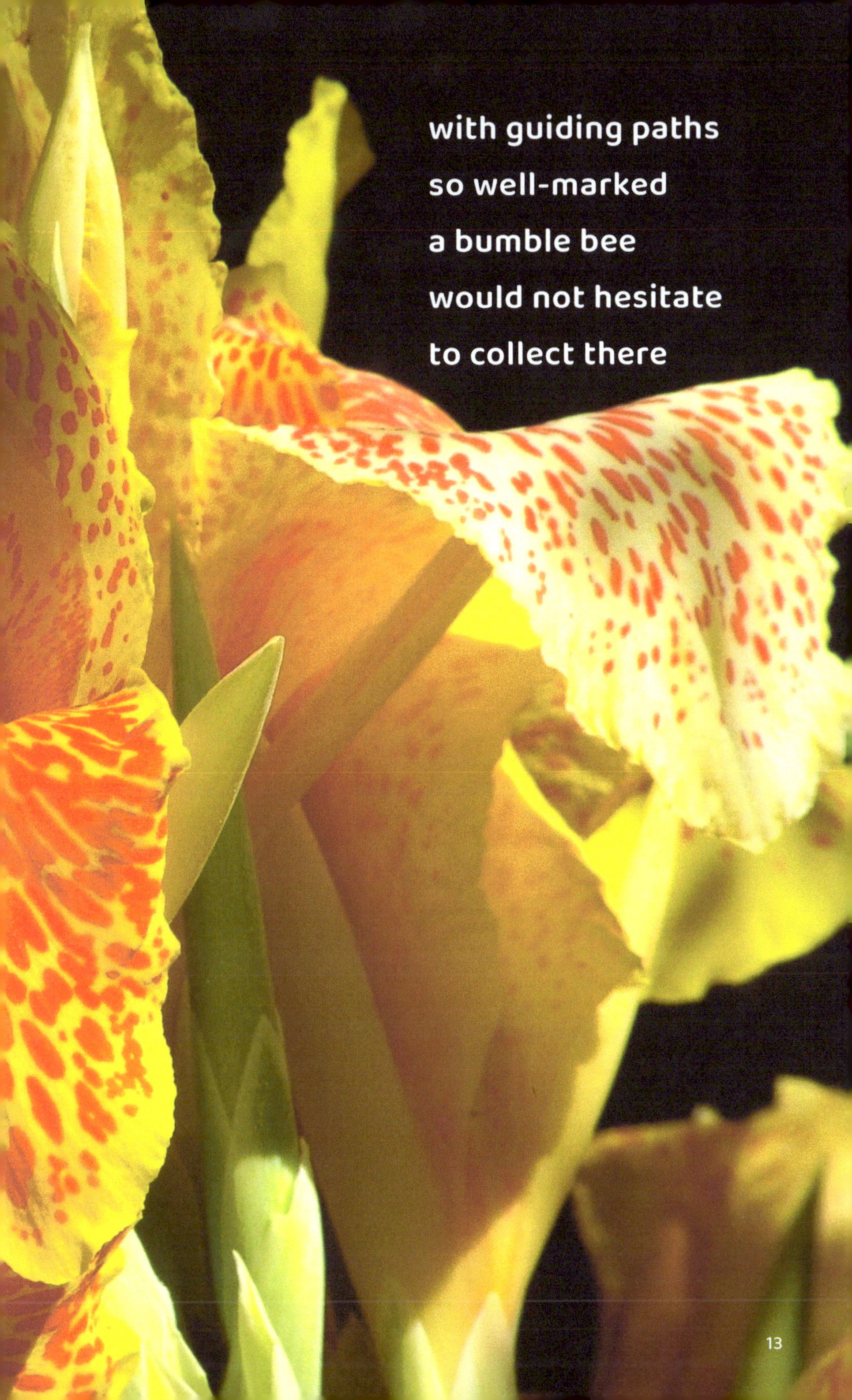

with guiding paths
so well-marked
a bumble bee
would not hesitate
to collect there

stages of life
sometimes can be seen
to overlap . . .
here, full-blossom and seed pod
stand straight as neighbors

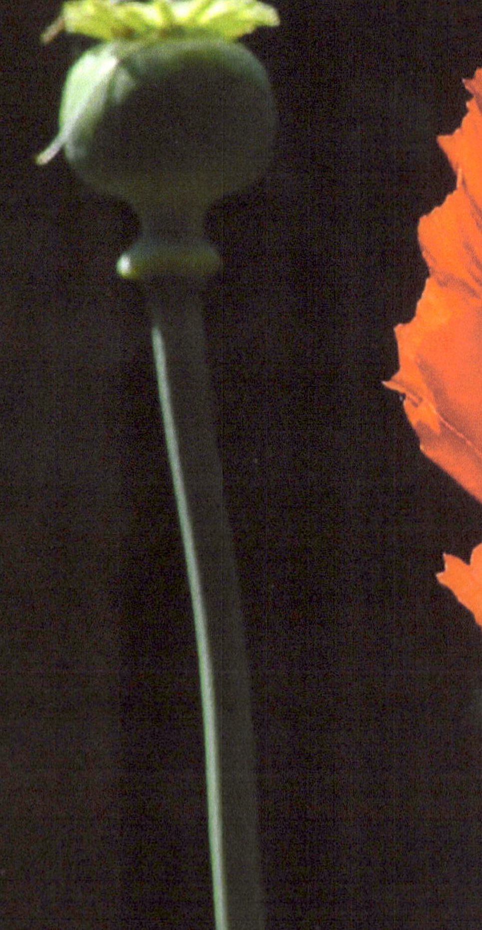

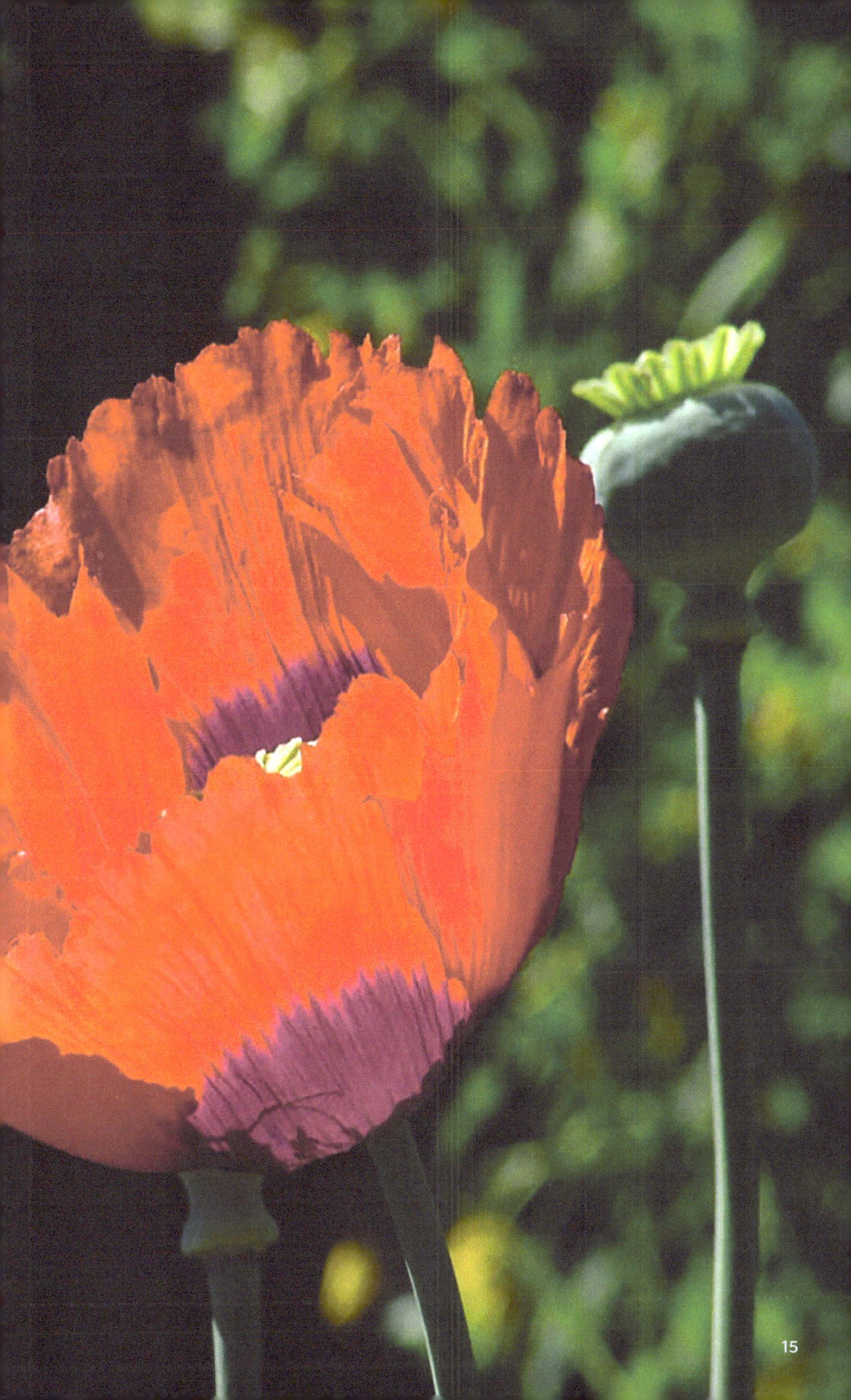

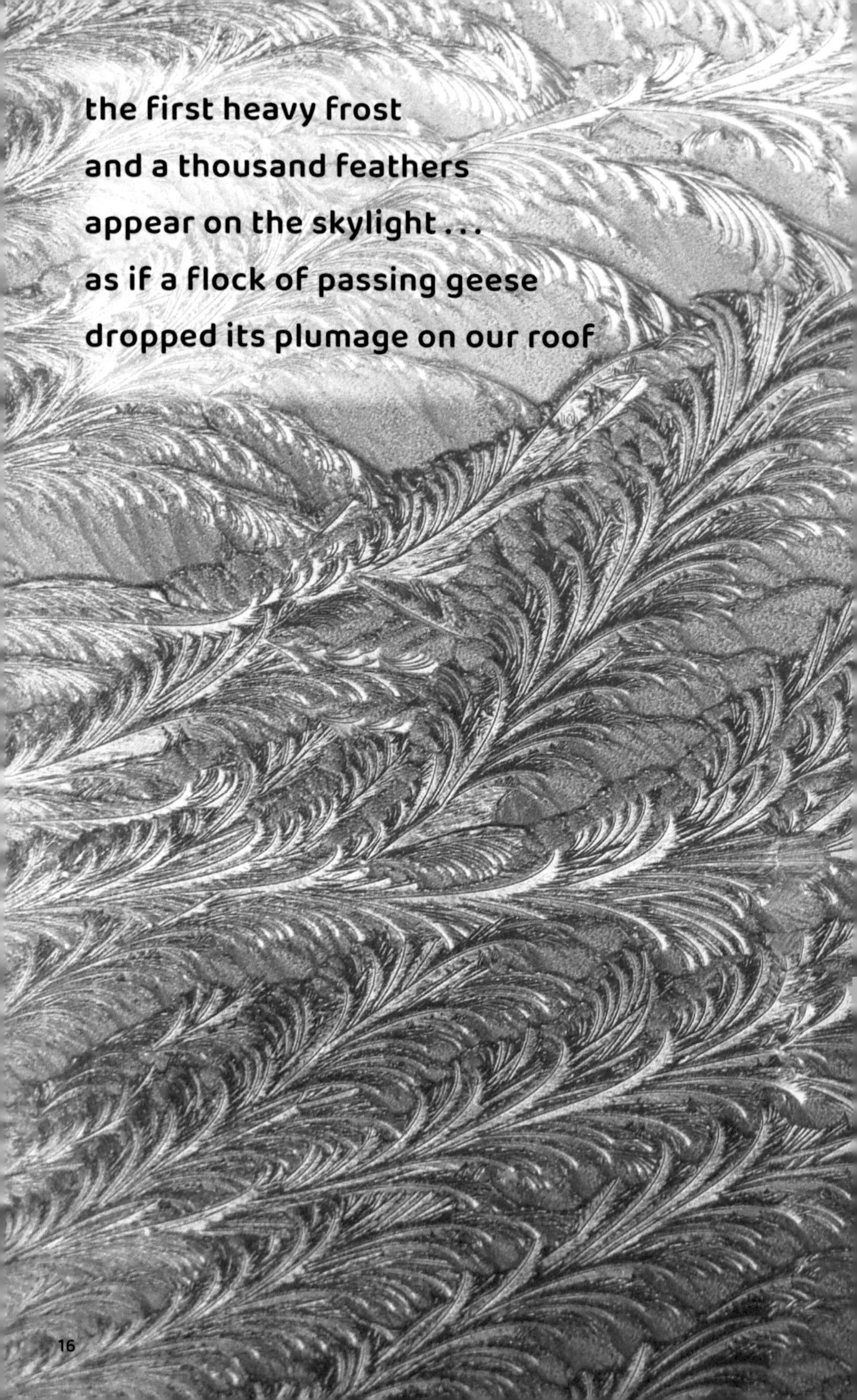

the first heavy frost
and a thousand feathers
appear on the skylight . . .
as if a flock of passing geese
dropped its plumage on our roof

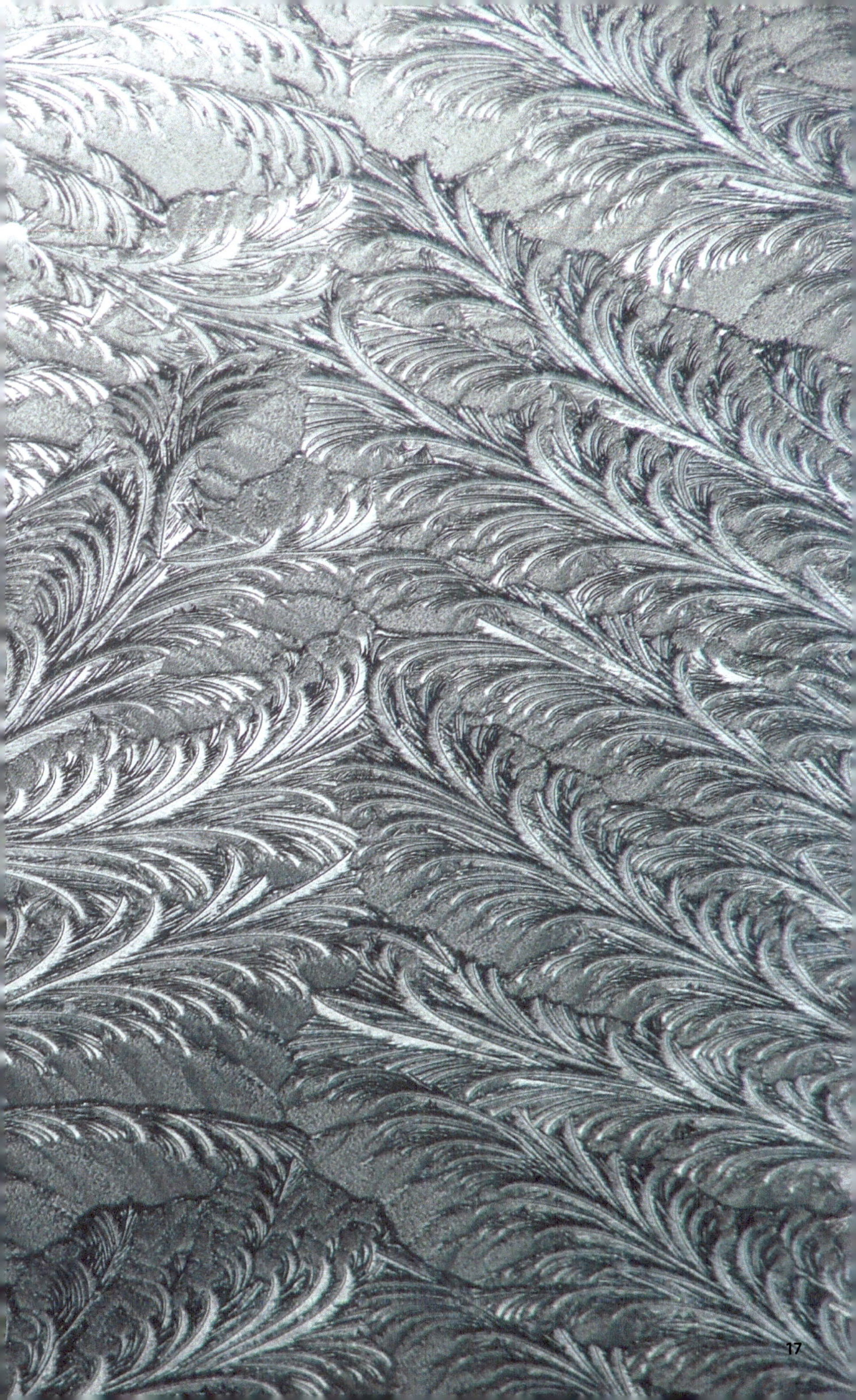

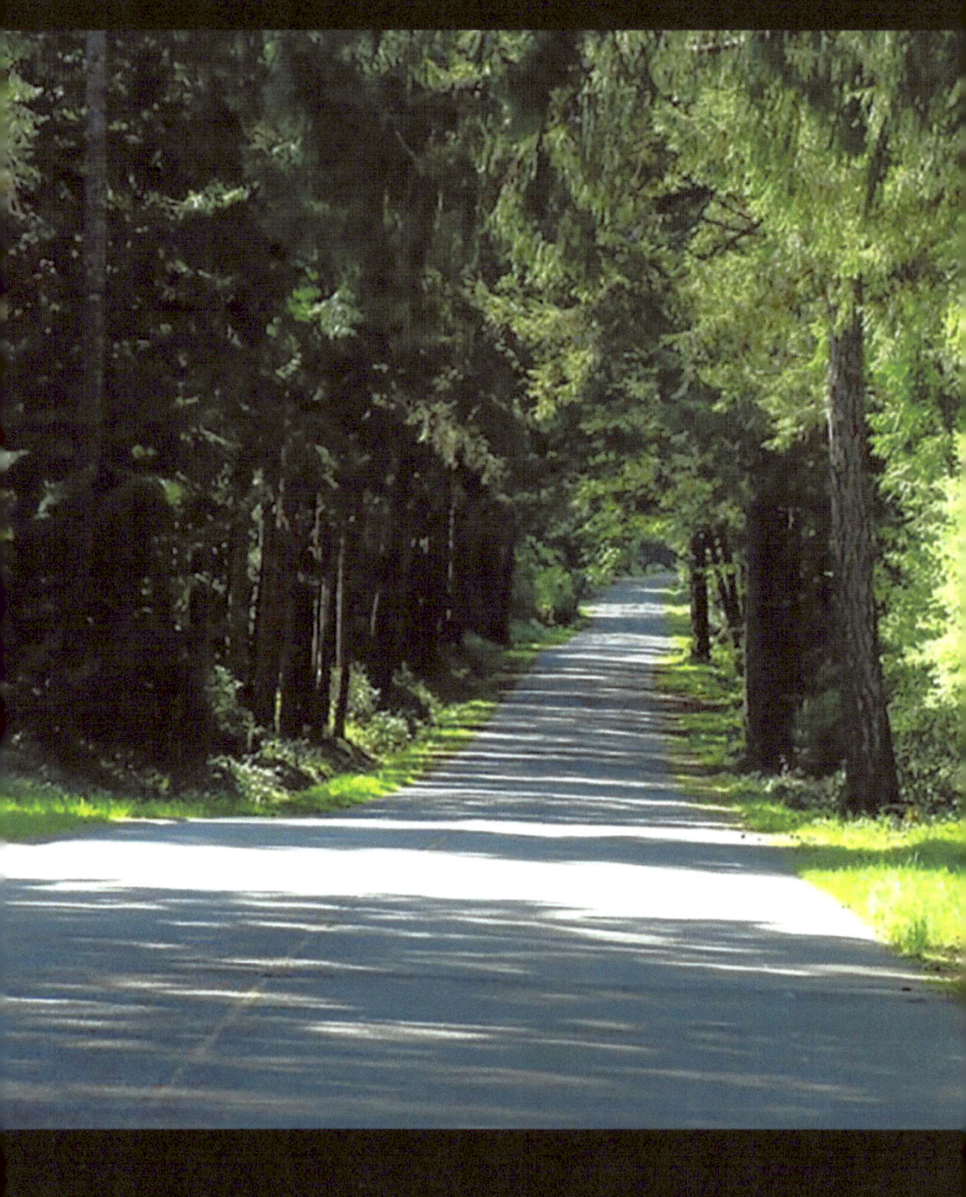

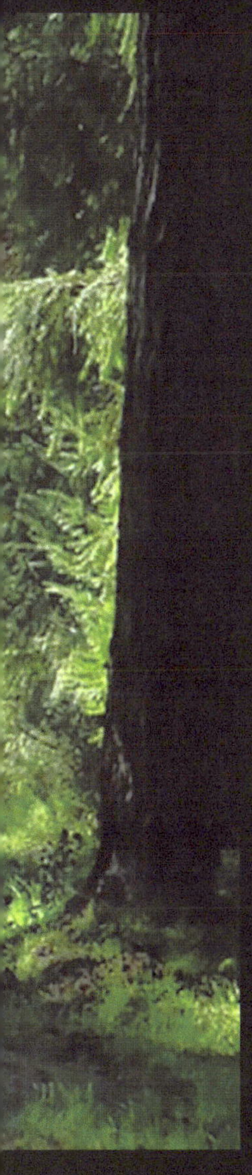

the tunnel
provides shade in summer,
a haunting place
for Halloween pumpkins
and snow-free driving later

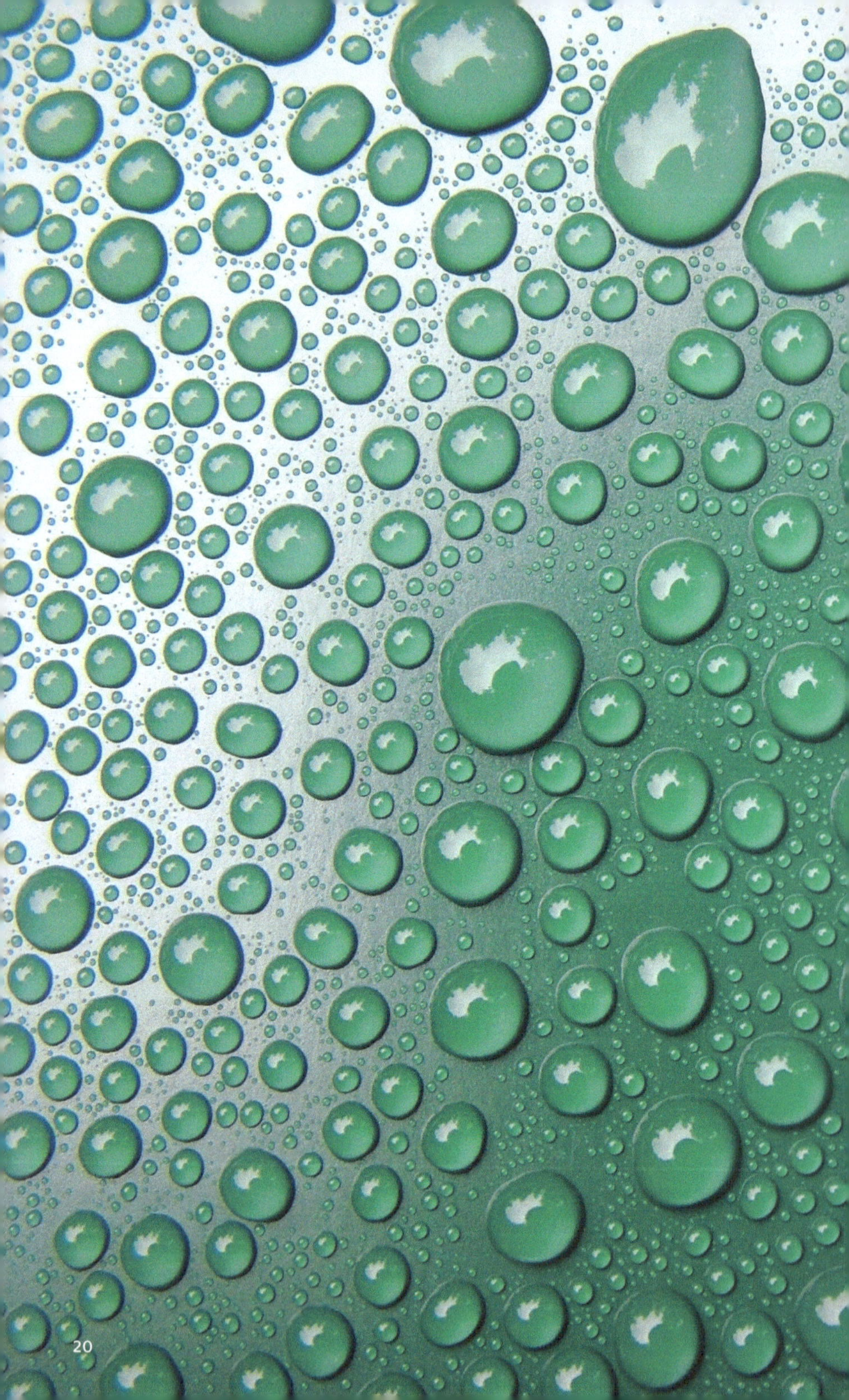

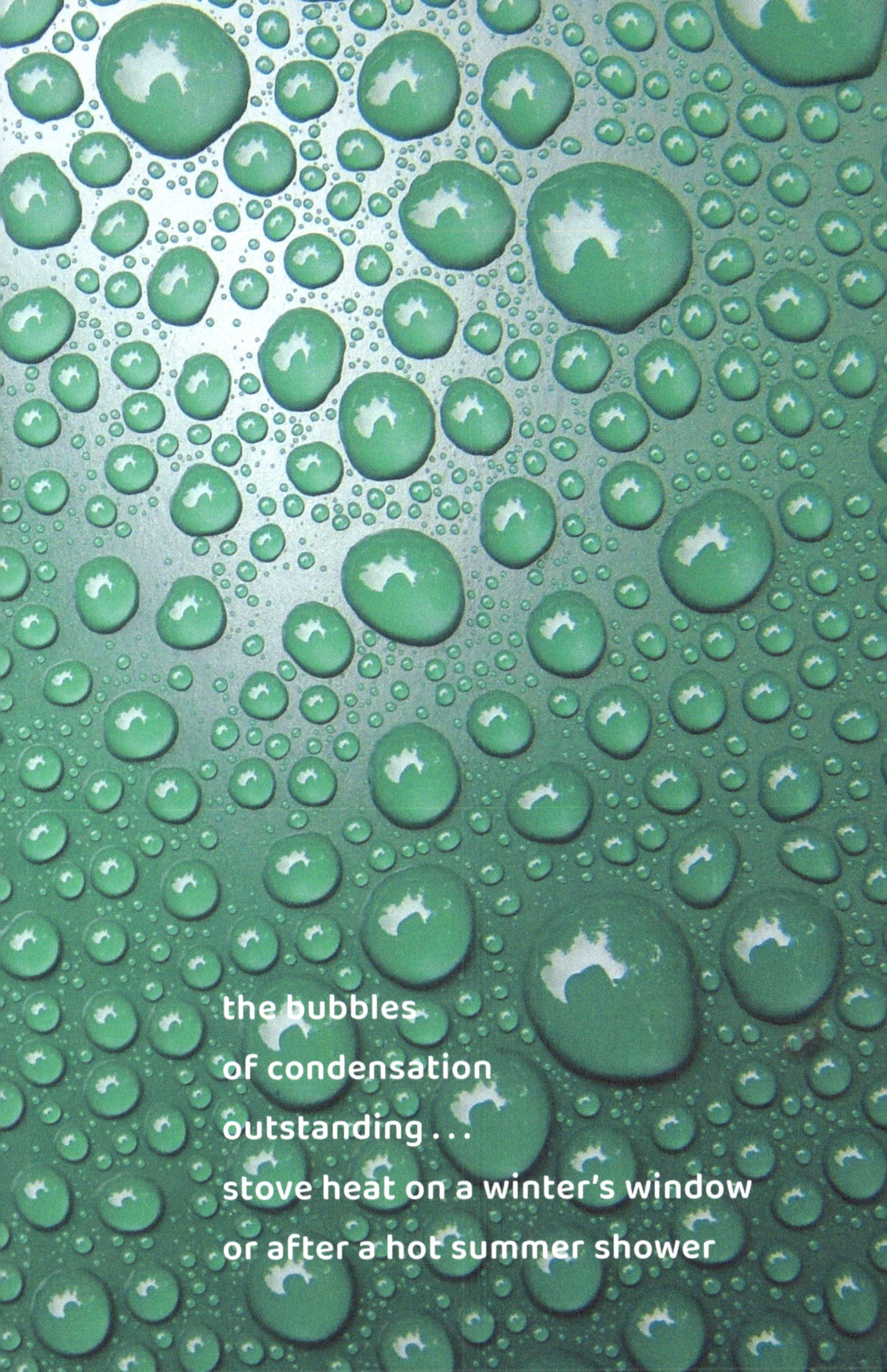

the bubbles
of condensation
outstanding . . .
stove heat on a winter's window
or after a hot summer shower

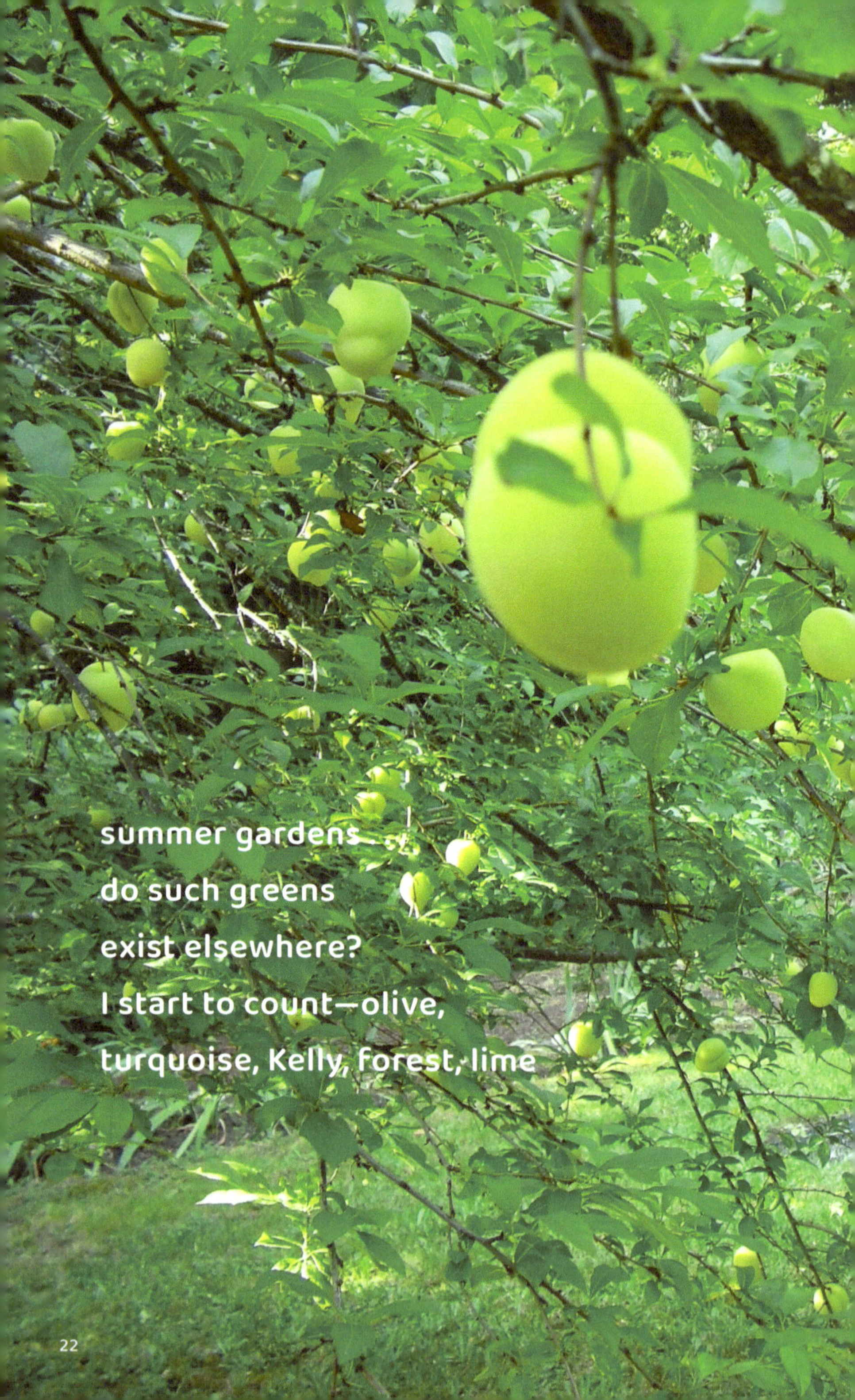

summer gardens . . .
do such greens
exist elsewhere?
I start to count—olive,
turquoise, Kelly, forest, lime

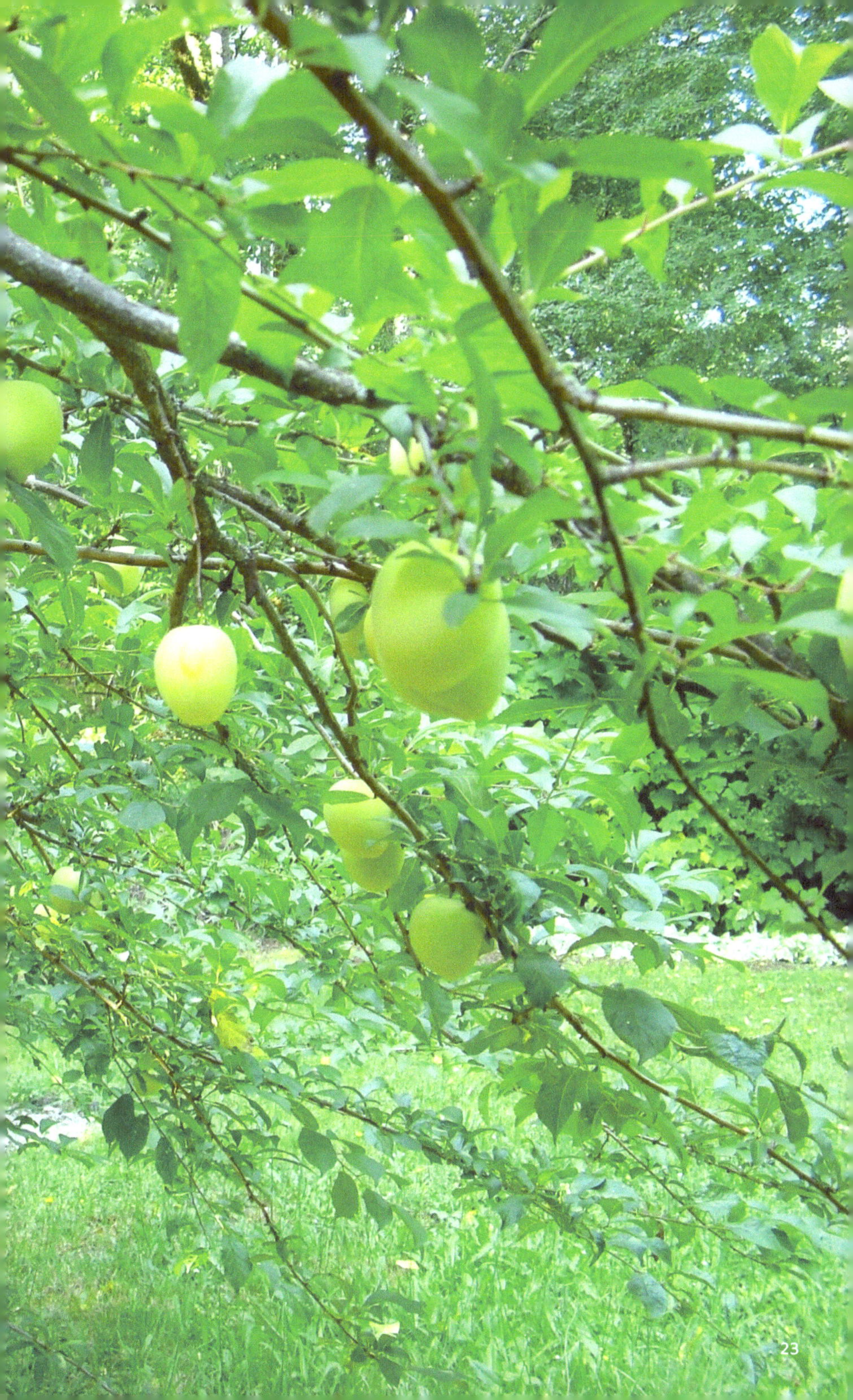

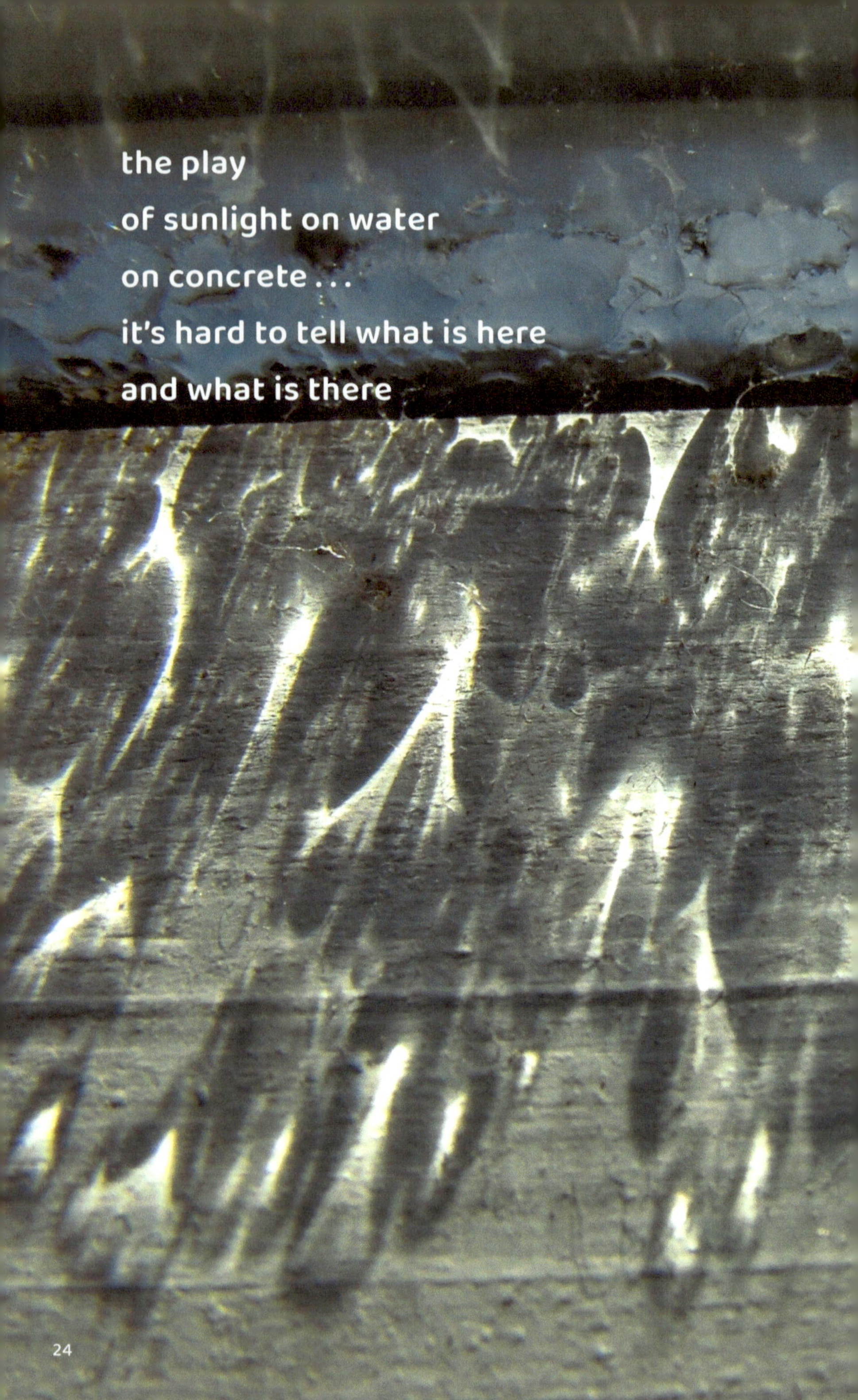

the play
of sunlight on water
on concrete . . .
it's hard to tell what is here
and what is there

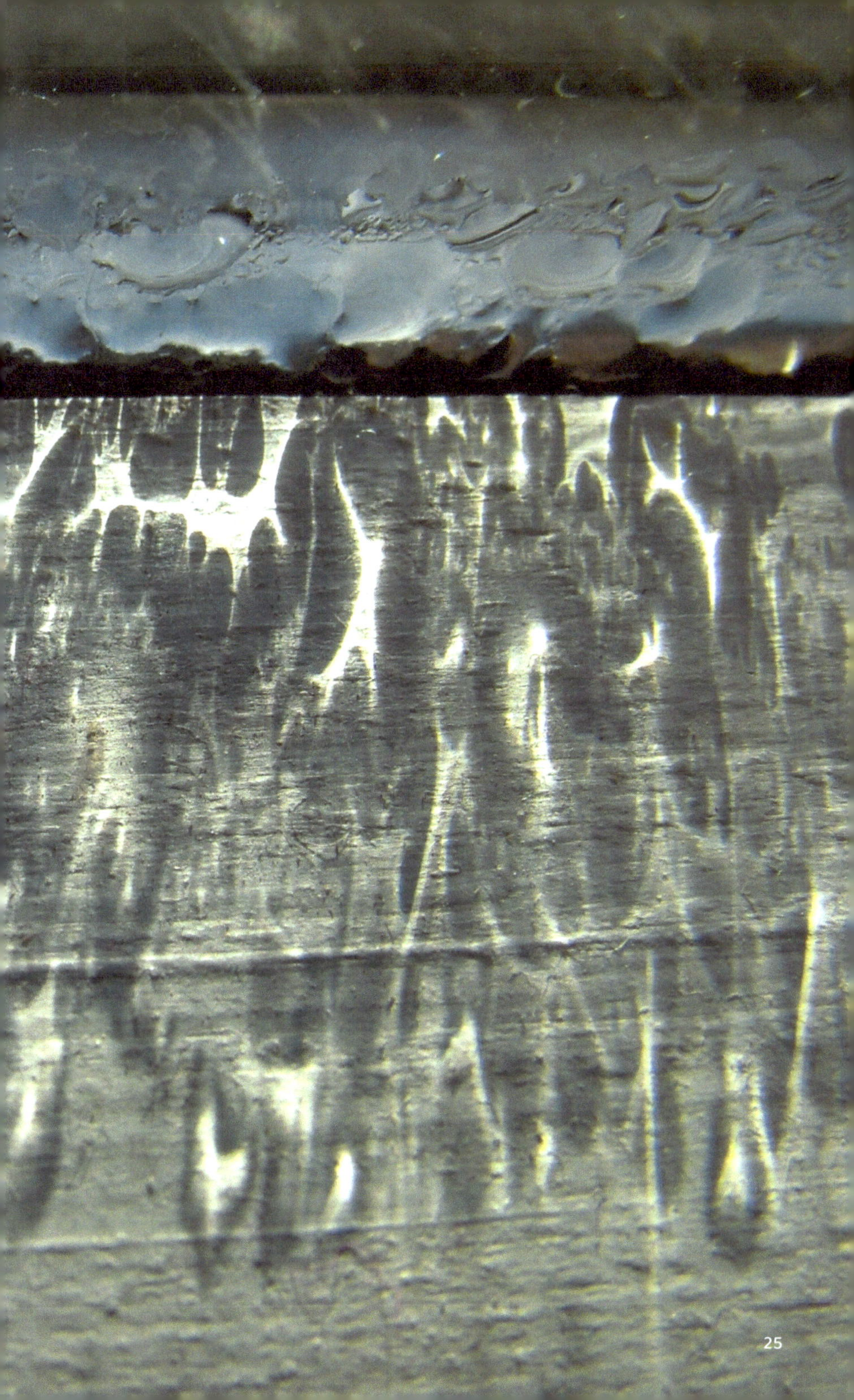

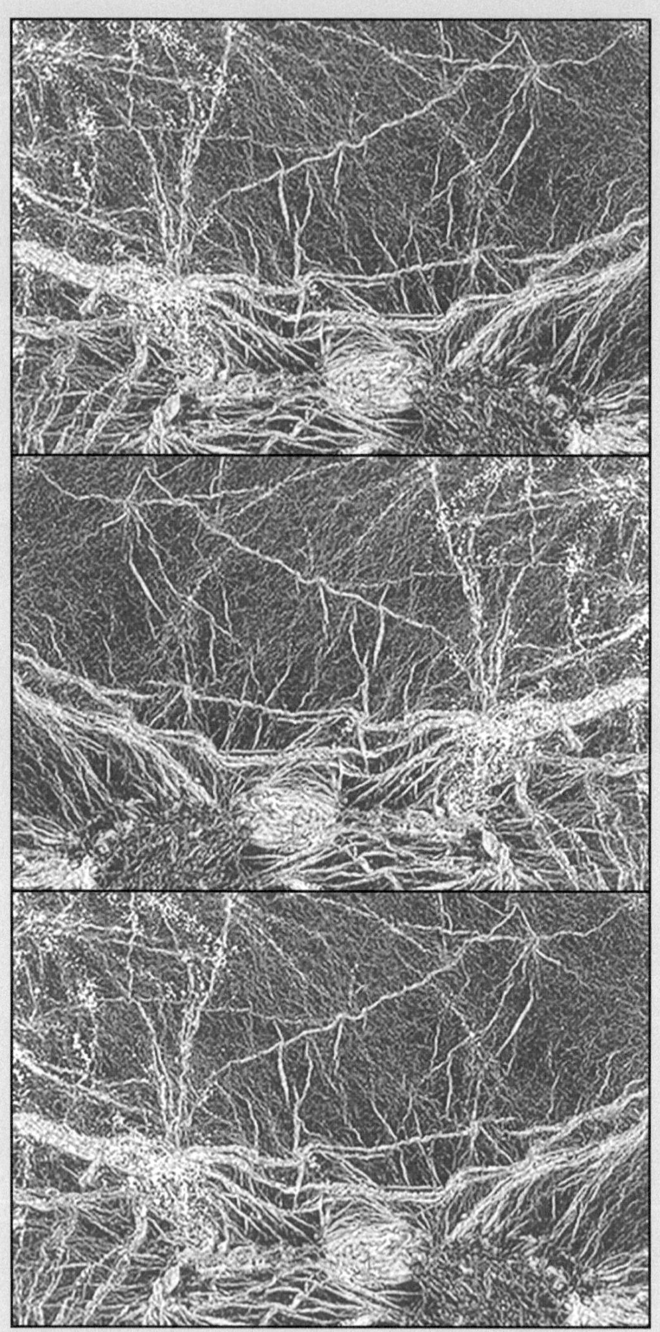

tidepools

hold a wealth

of life

that twice a day

get tidal swamping

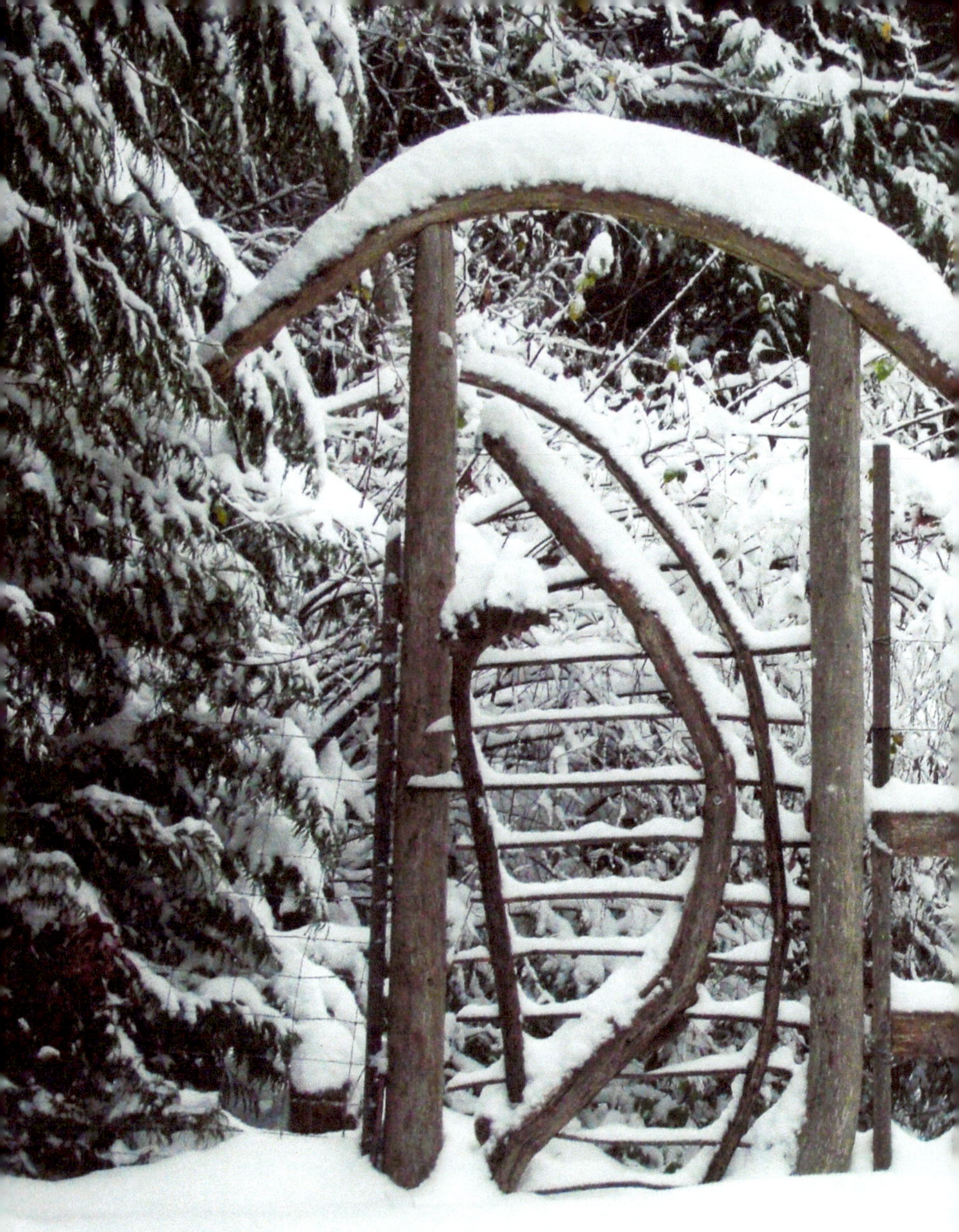

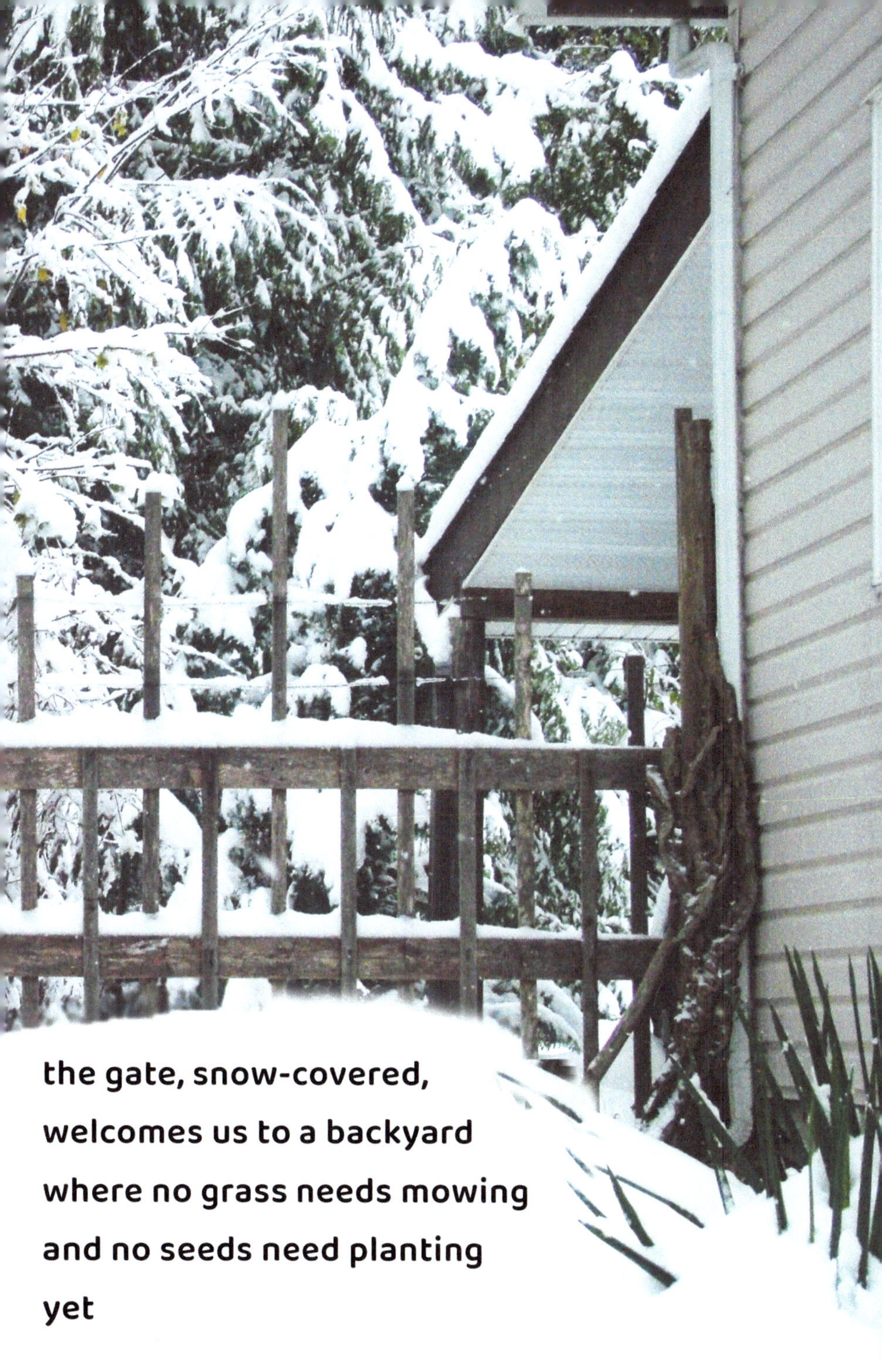

the gate, snow-covered,
welcomes us to a backyard
where no grass needs mowing
and no seeds need planting
yet

the otters nuzzle
on the rocks, not caring
that we
with our cameras
record their goings-on

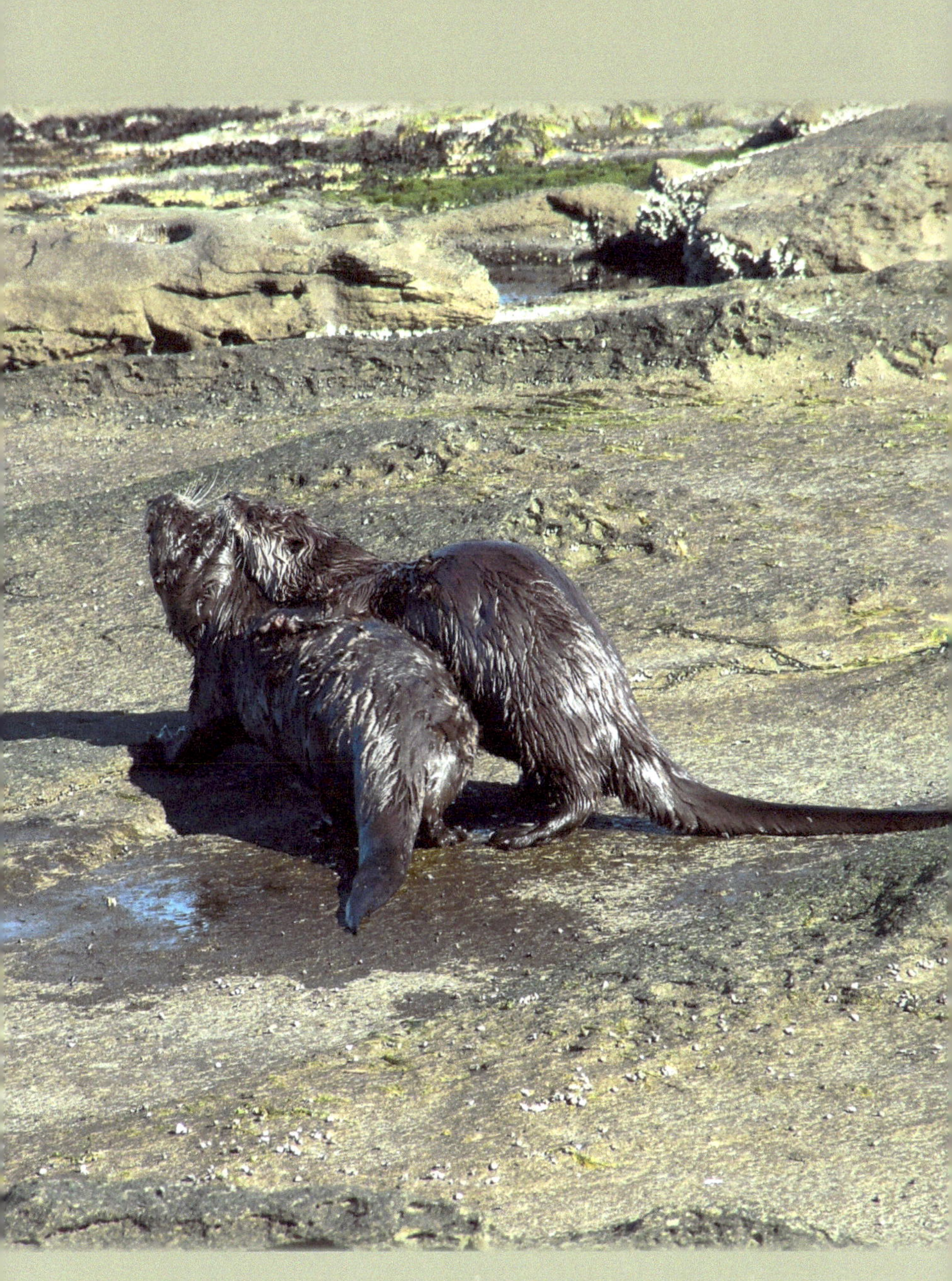

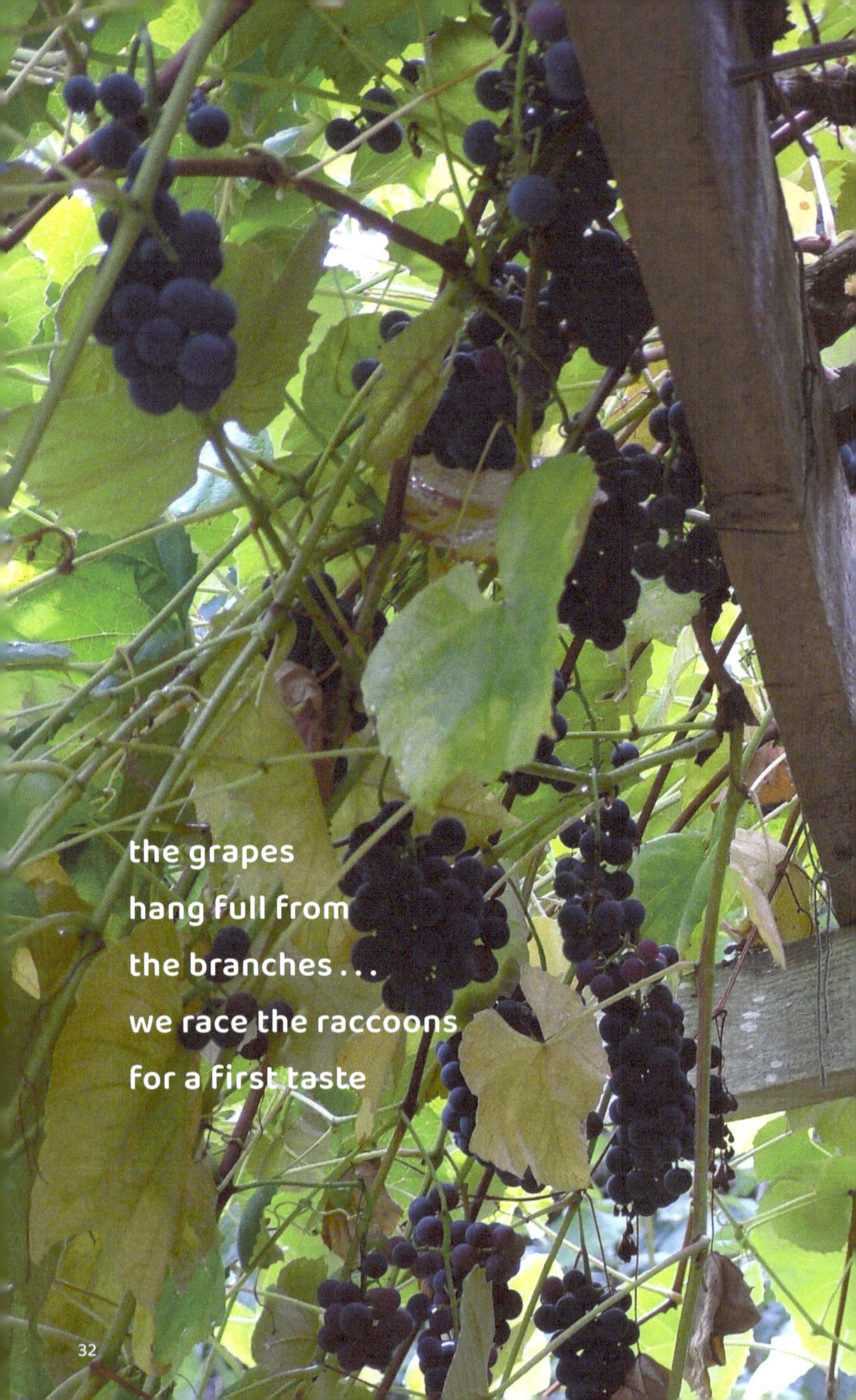

the grapes
hang full from
the branches . . .
we race the raccoons
for a first taste

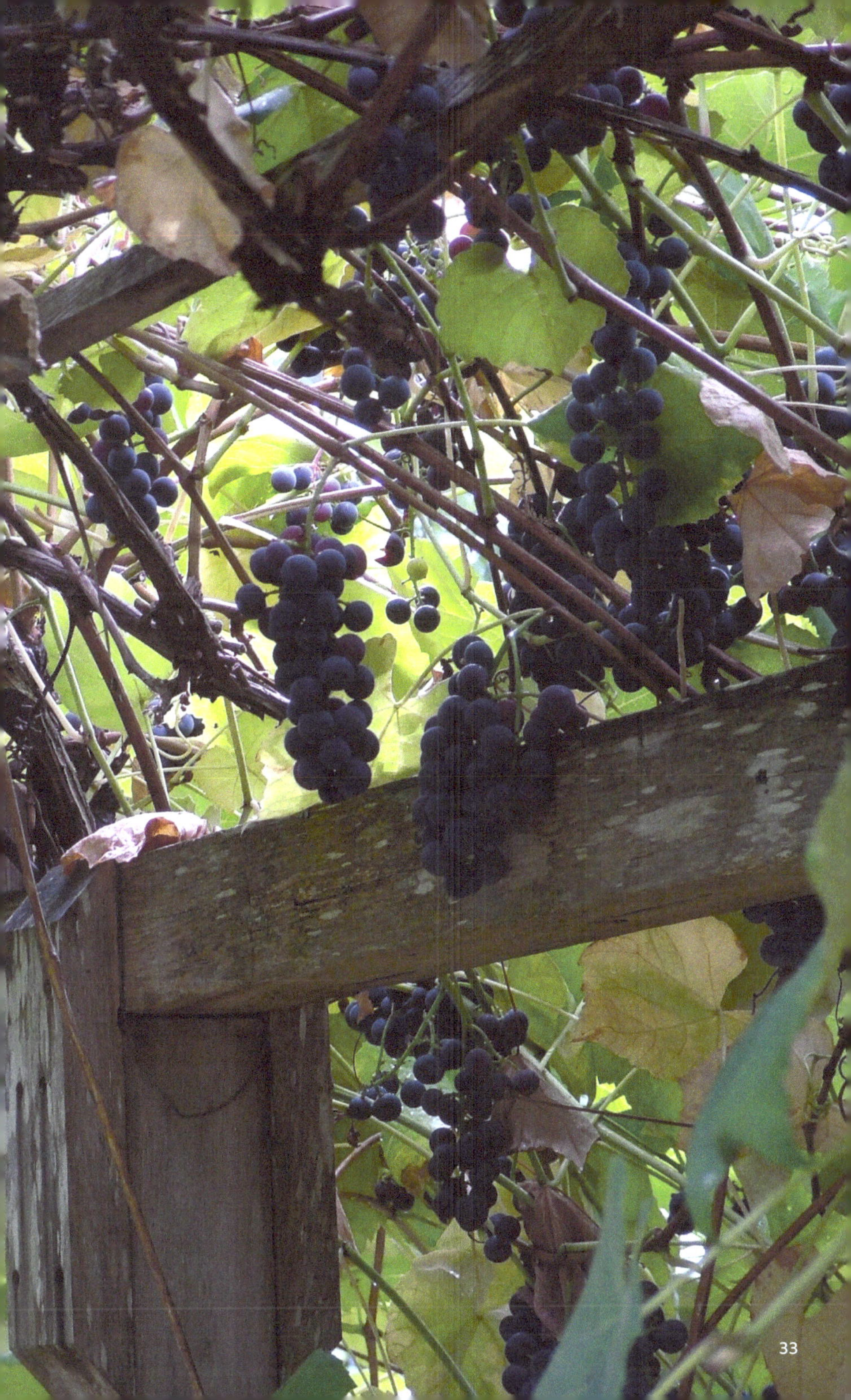

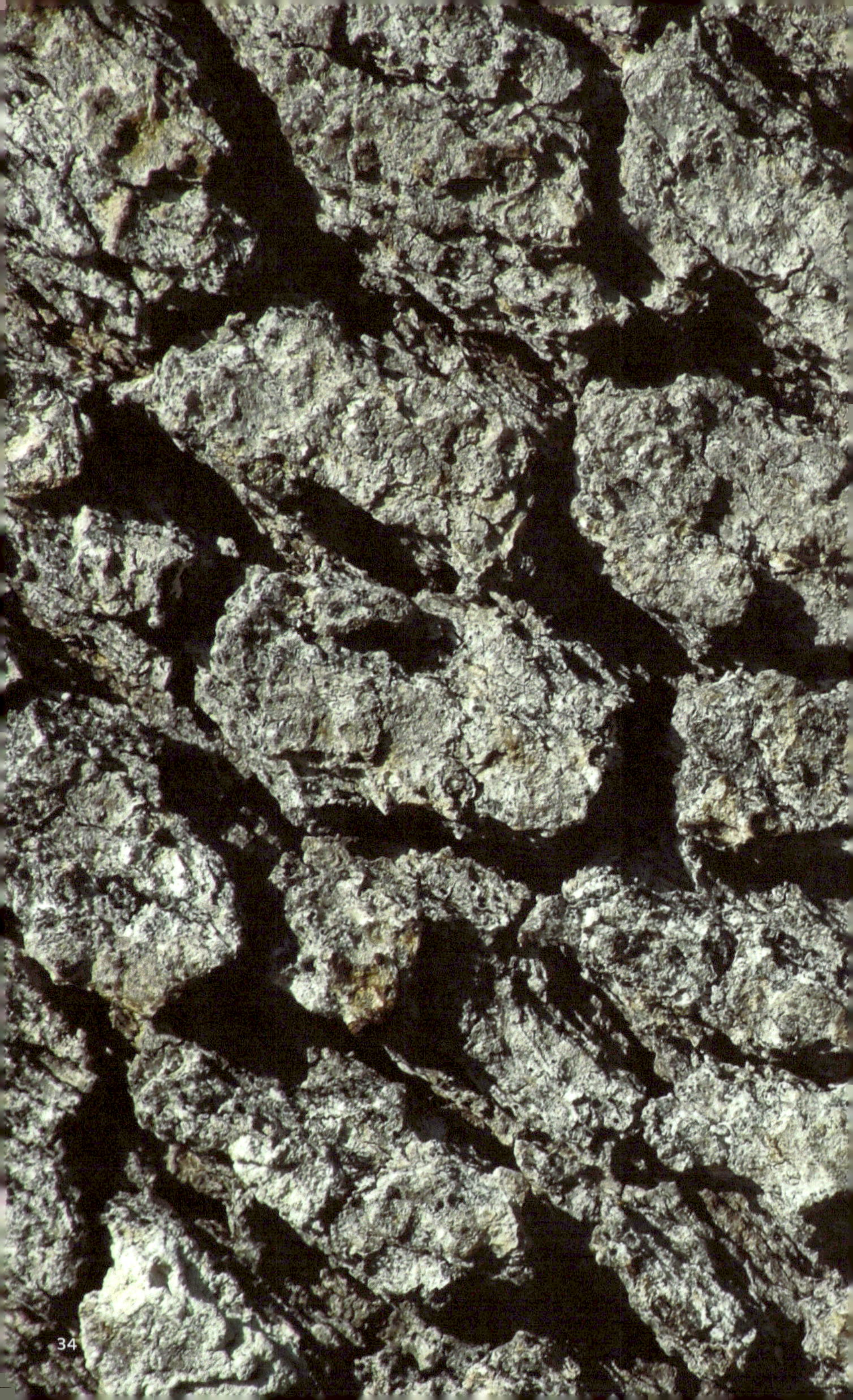

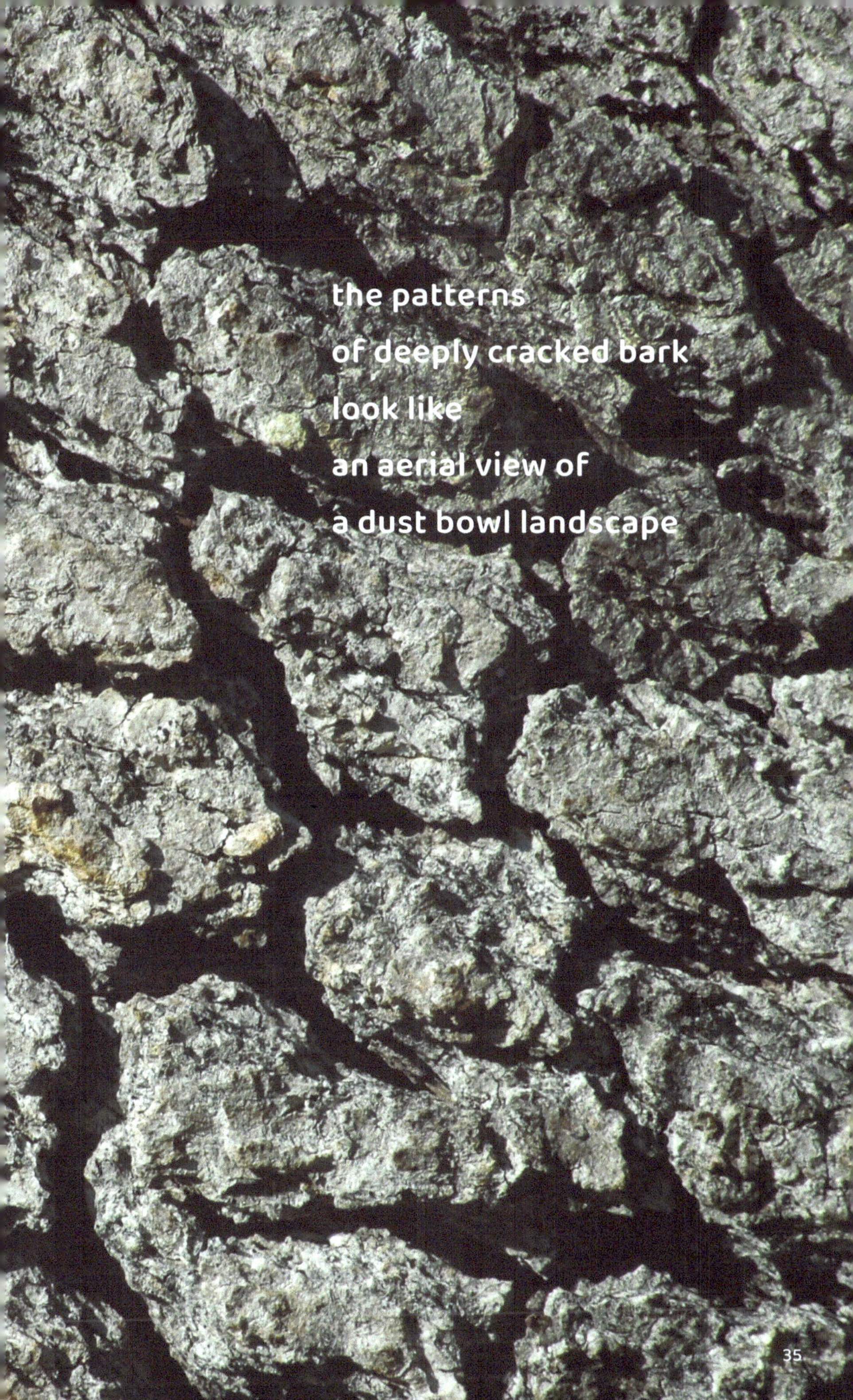

the patterns
of deeply cracked bark
look like
an aerial view of
a dust bowl landscape

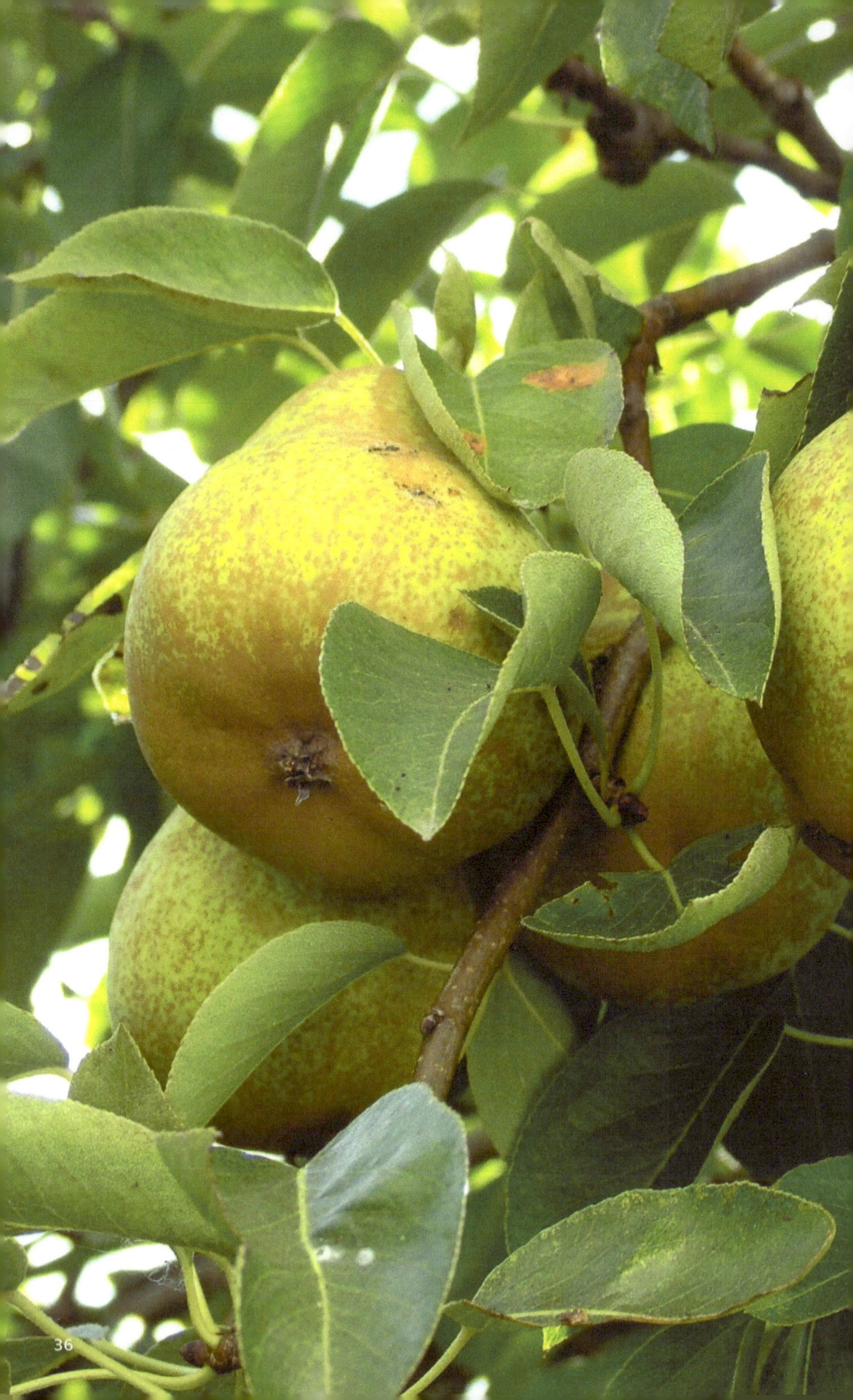

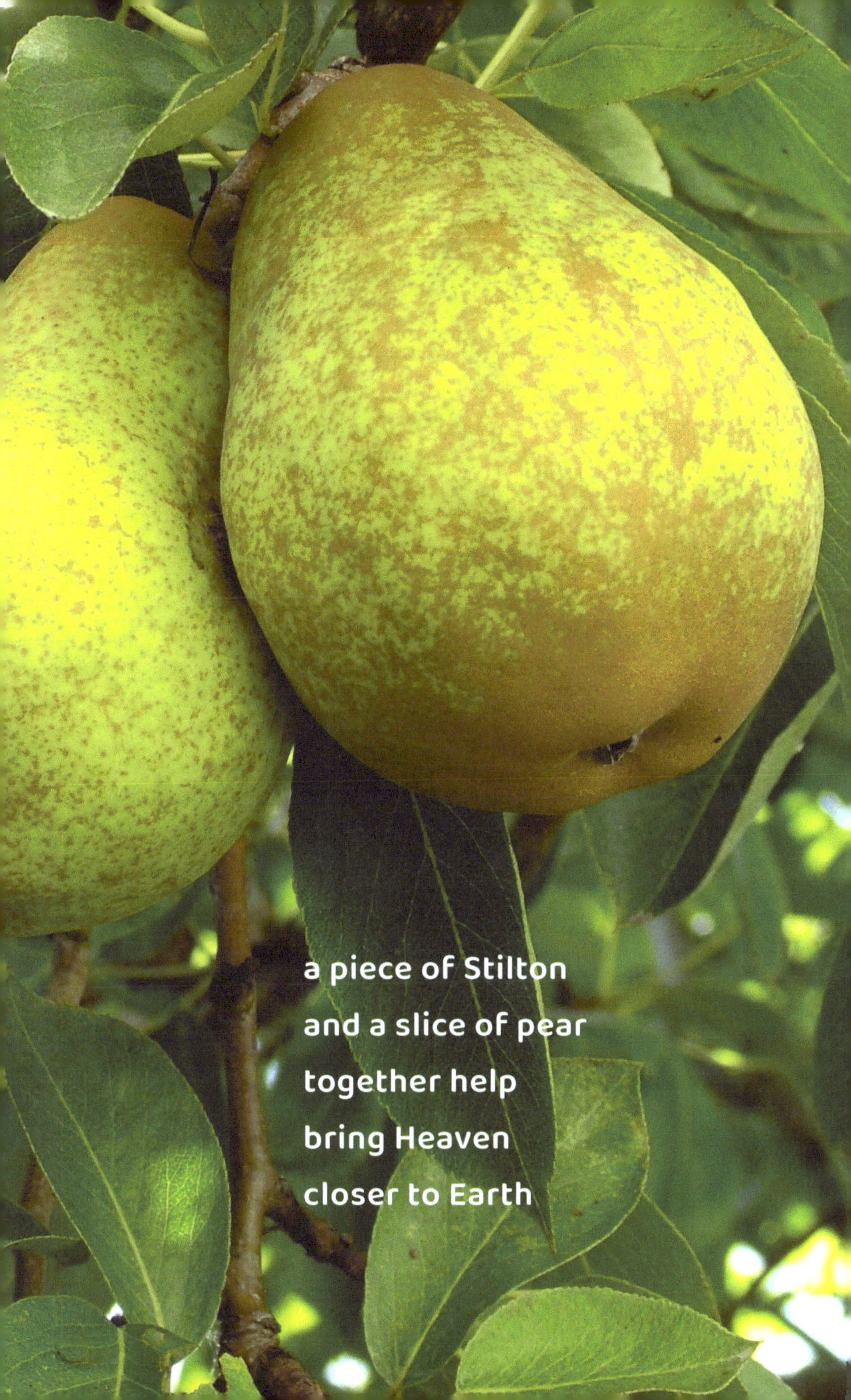
a piece of Stilton
and a slice of pear
together help
bring Heaven
closer to Earth

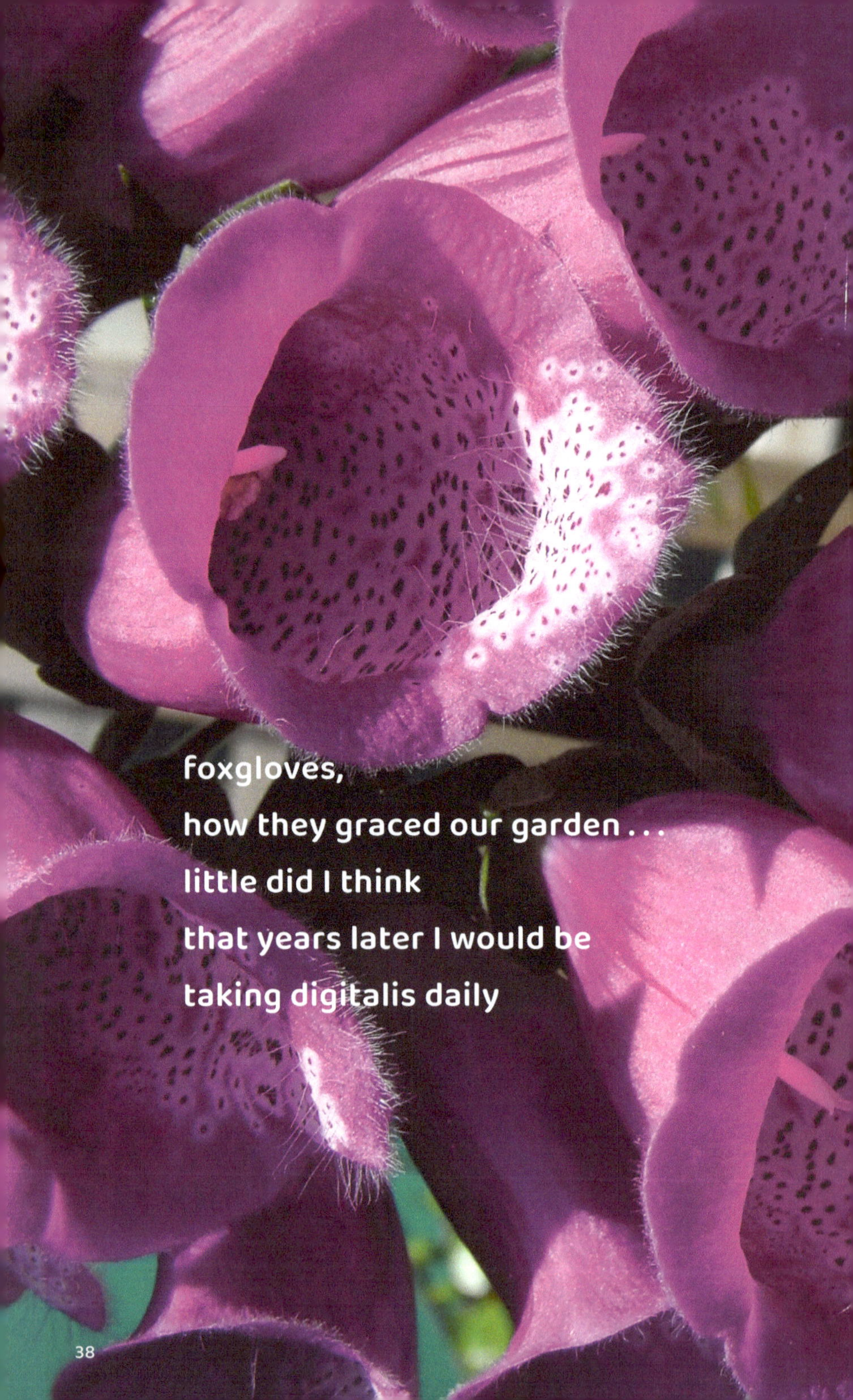

foxgloves,
how they graced our garden . . .
little did I think
that years later I would be
taking digitalis daily

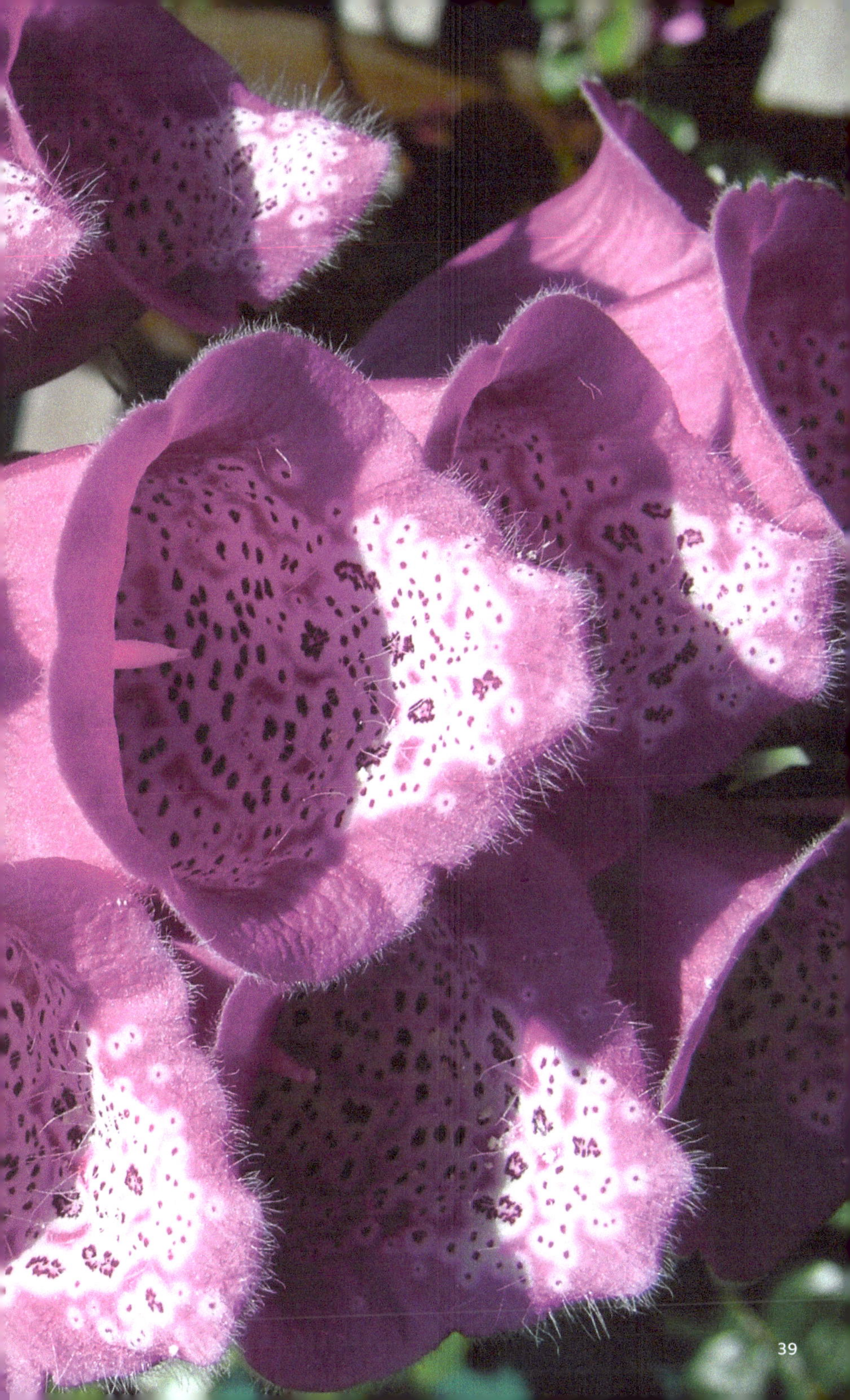

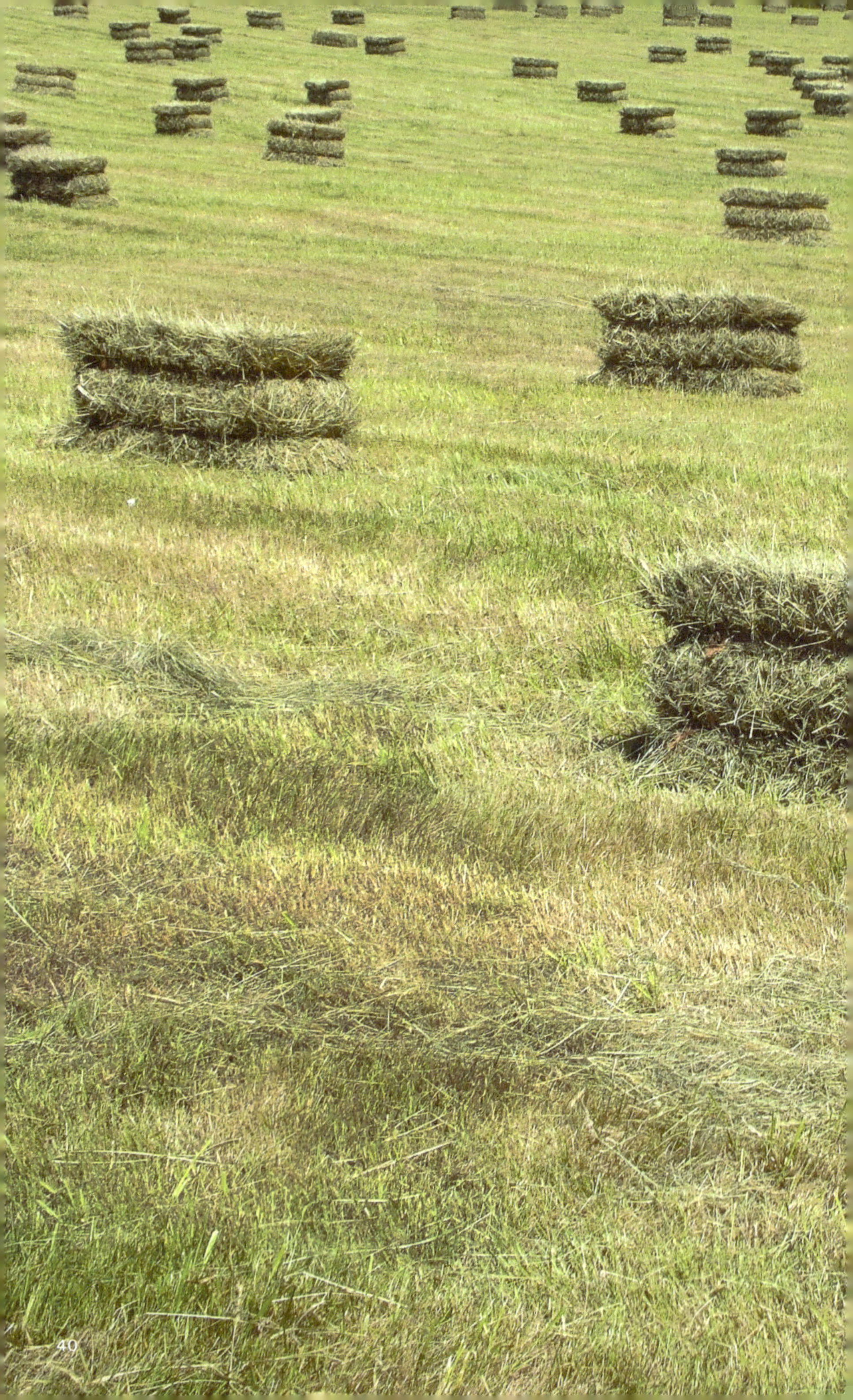

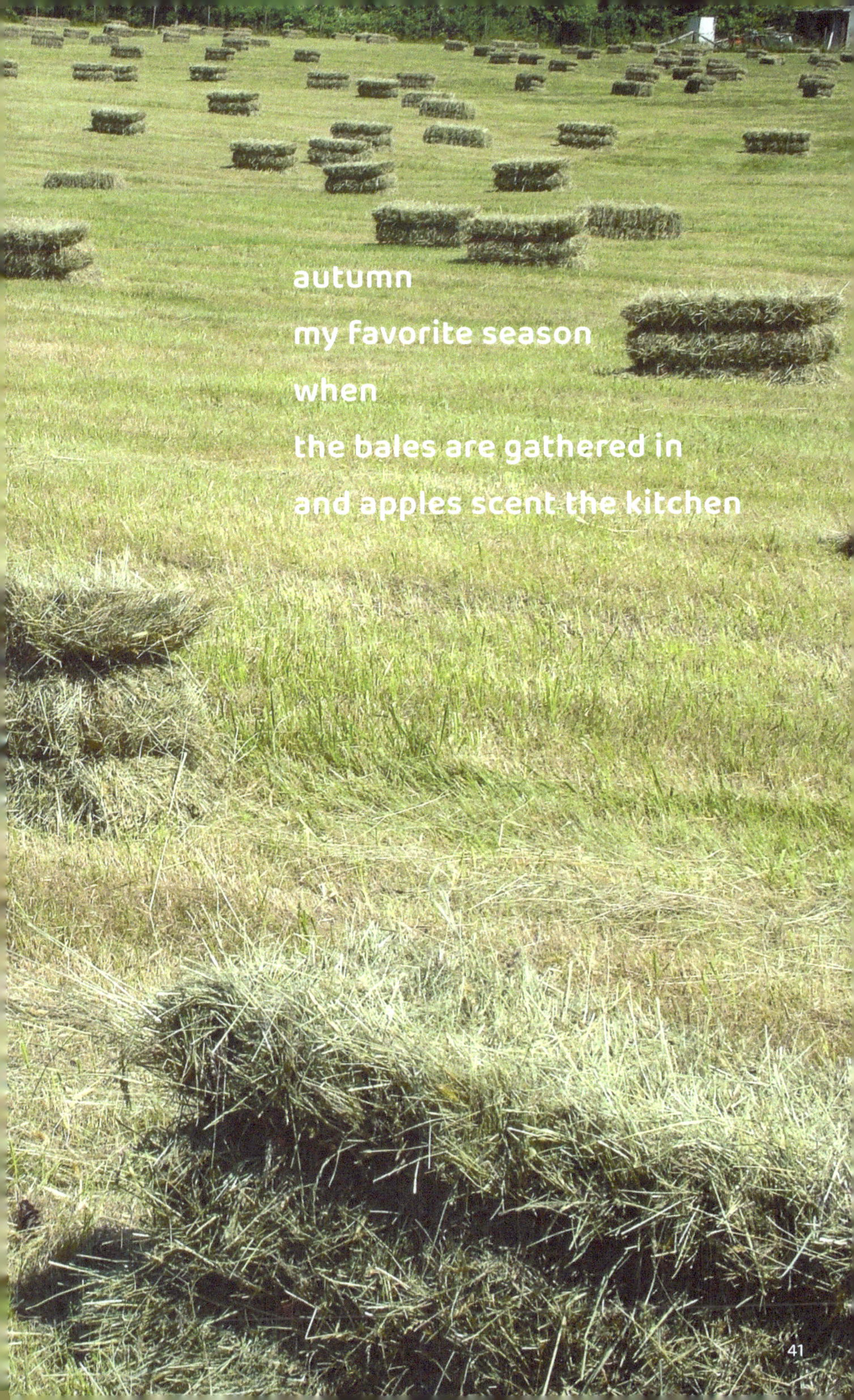

autumn
my favorite season
when
the bales are gathered in
and apples scent the kitchen

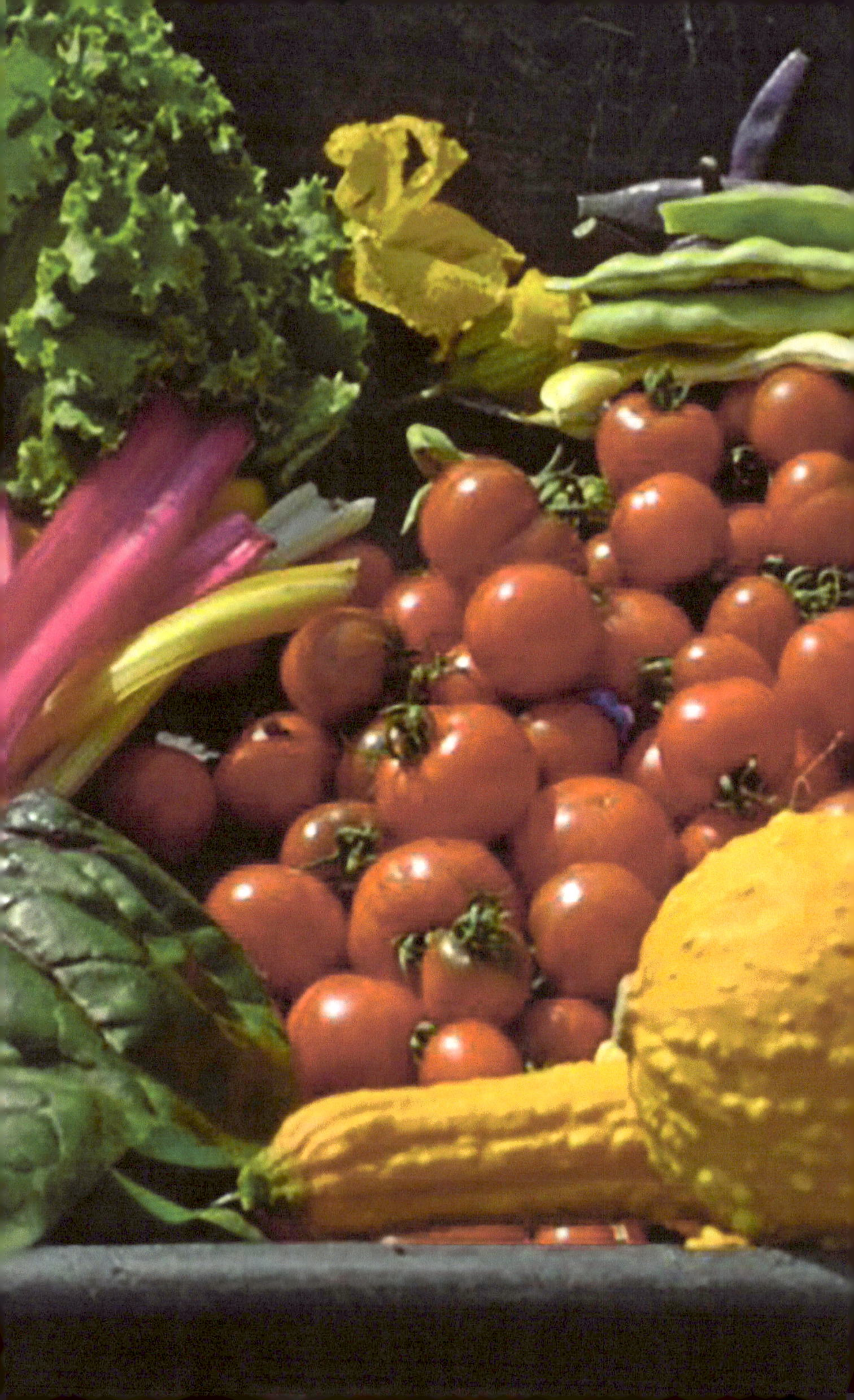

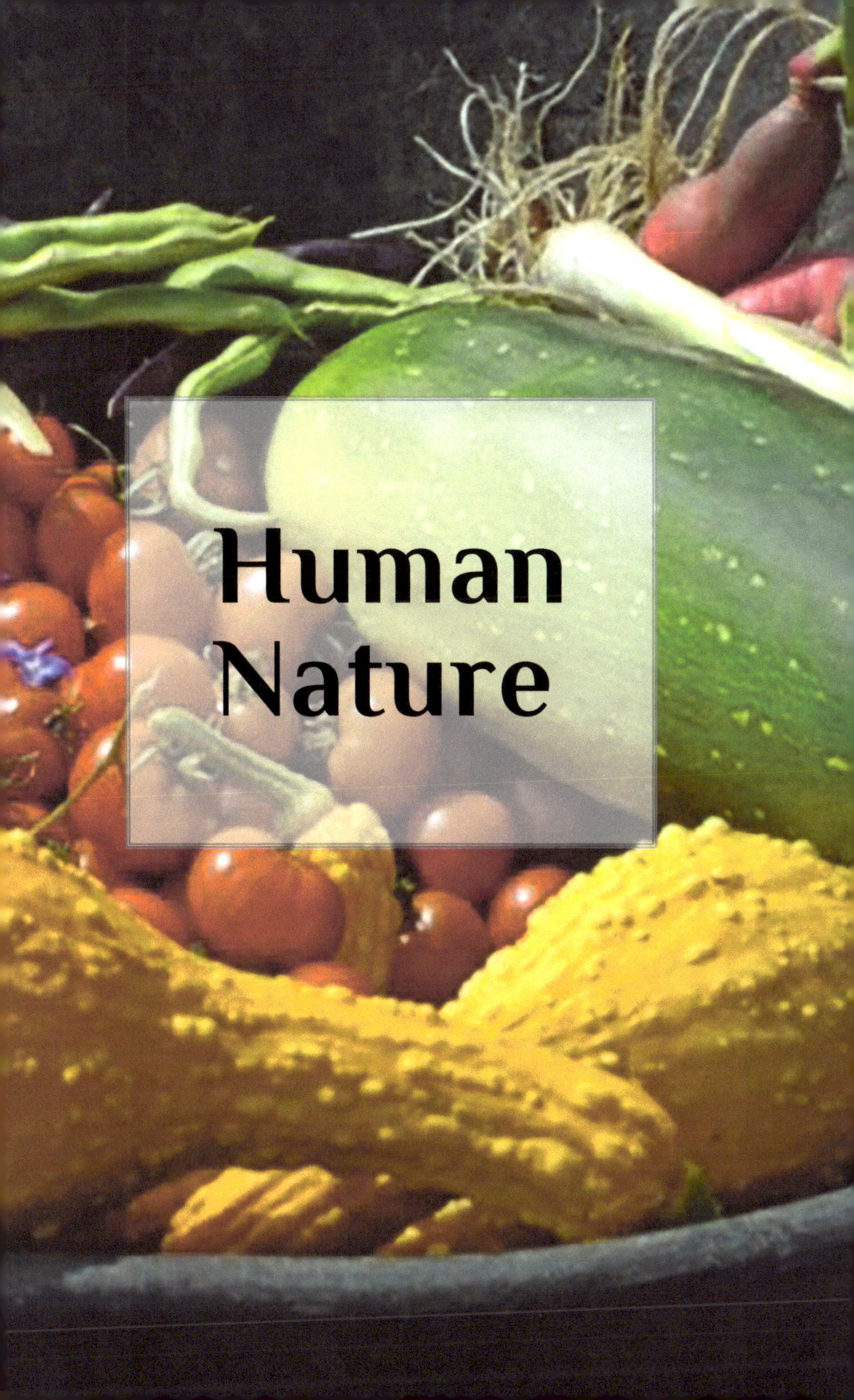
Human
Nature

as she tells him
of her love, he bends down
to kiss her . . .
it's all so easy, why didn't
she think to do it days ago?

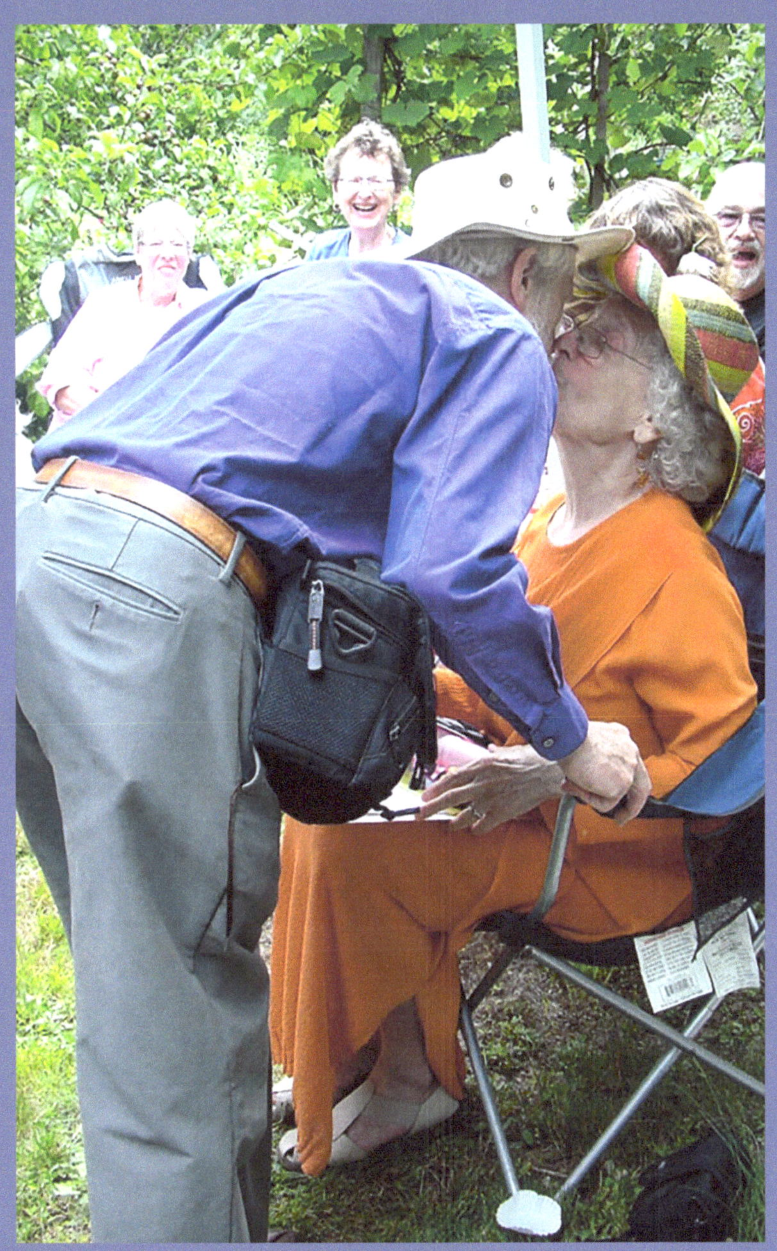

my total life
a shadow flickering
across the moon
one moment here
the next I float away

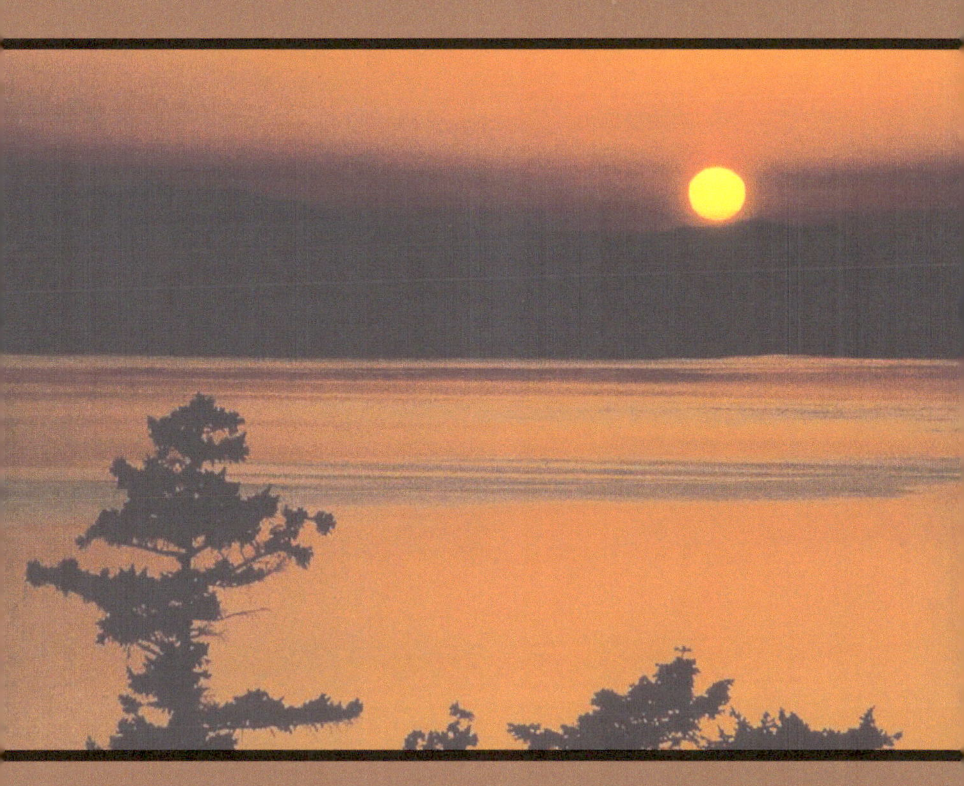

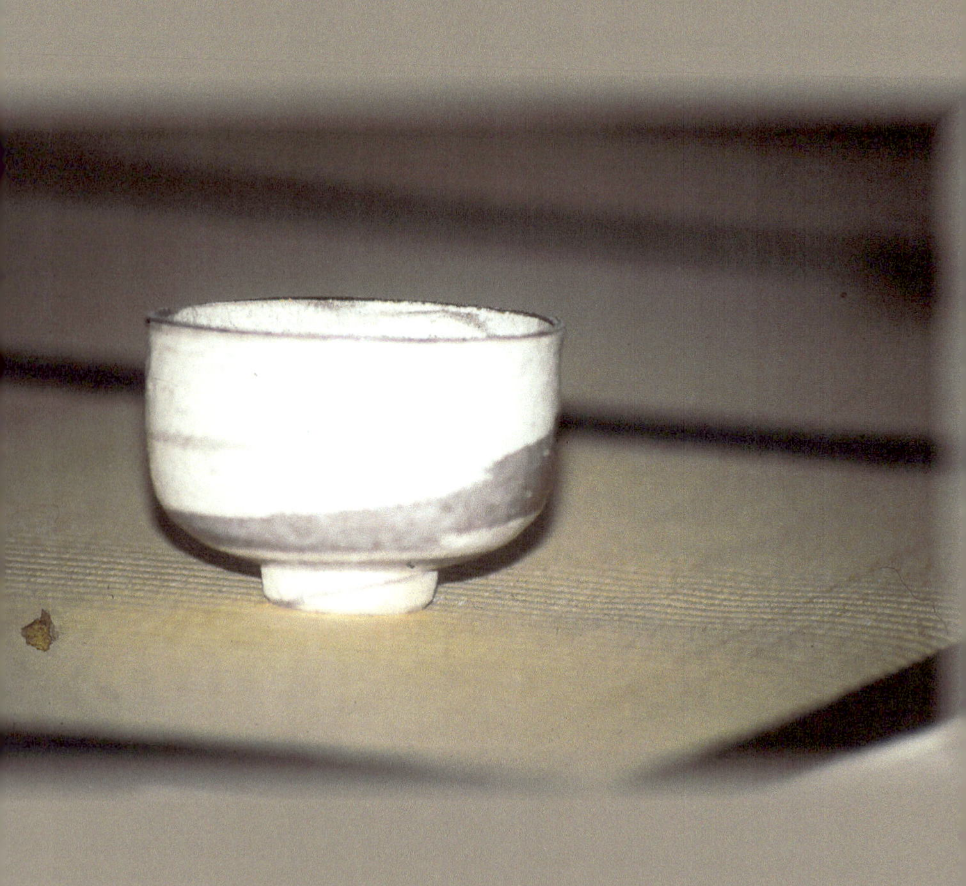

to reach an age

when things fall away

unneeded

as spent petals from a flower

as skins of summer snakes

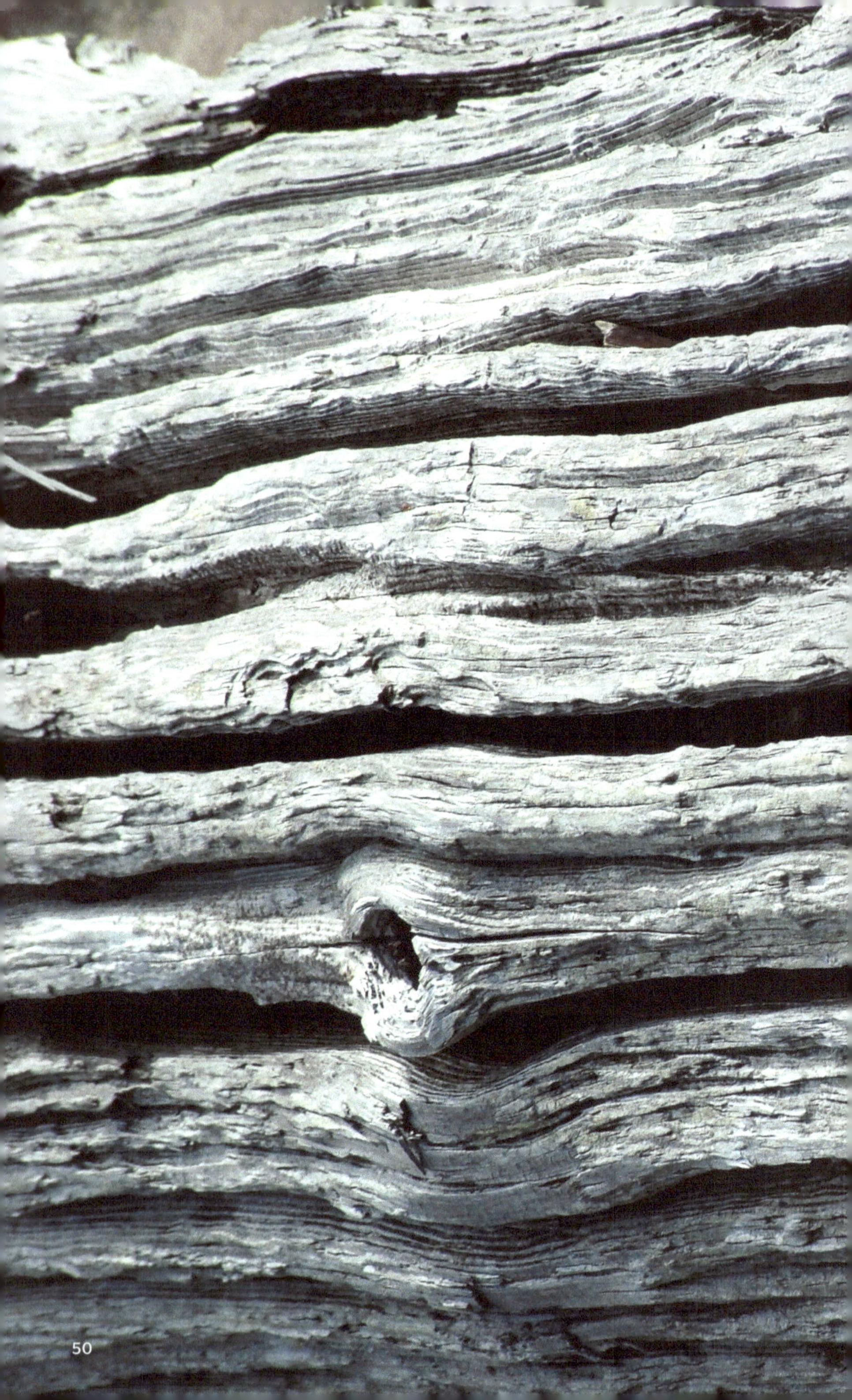

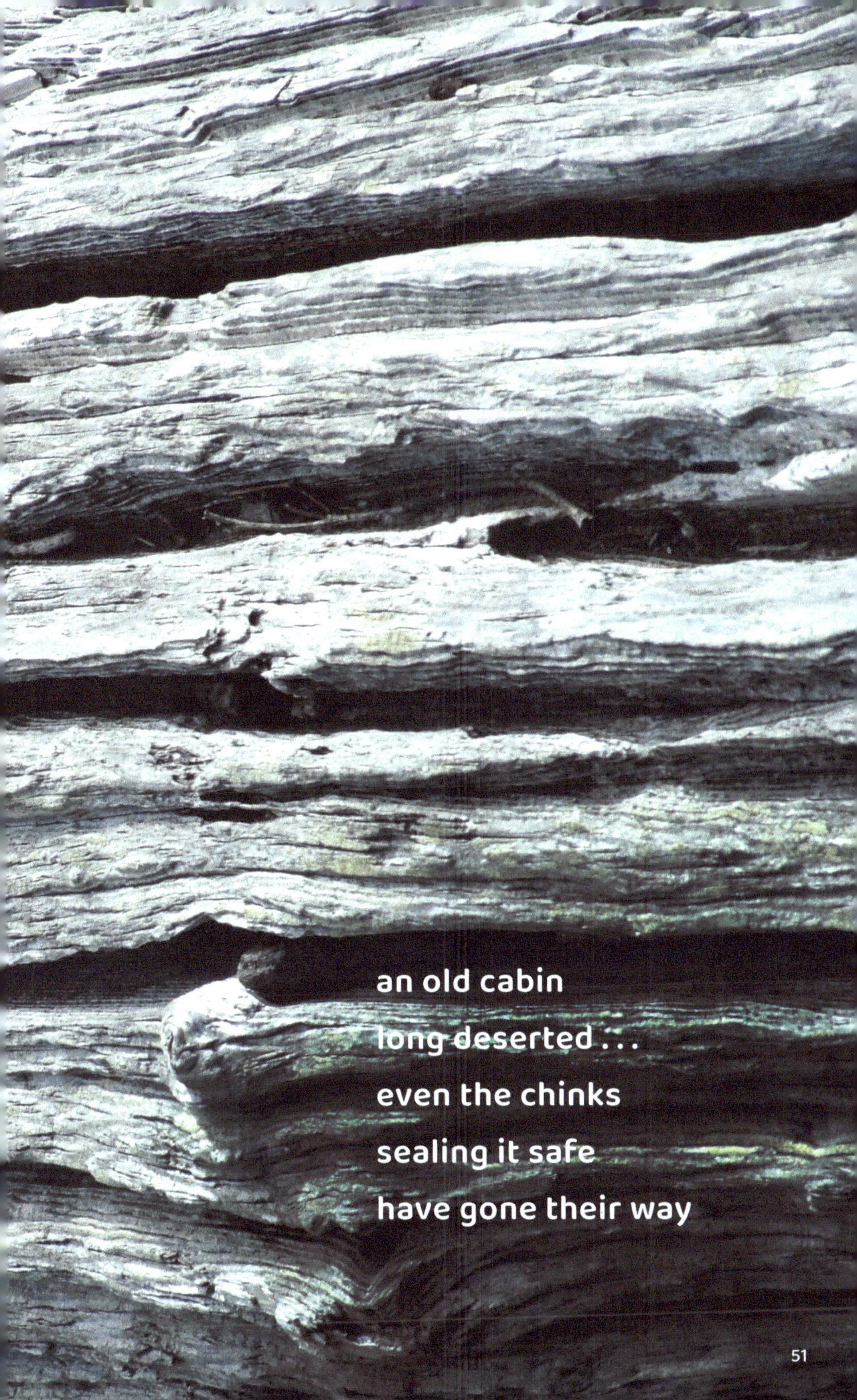

an old cabin
long deserted . . .
even the chinks
sealing it safe
have gone their way

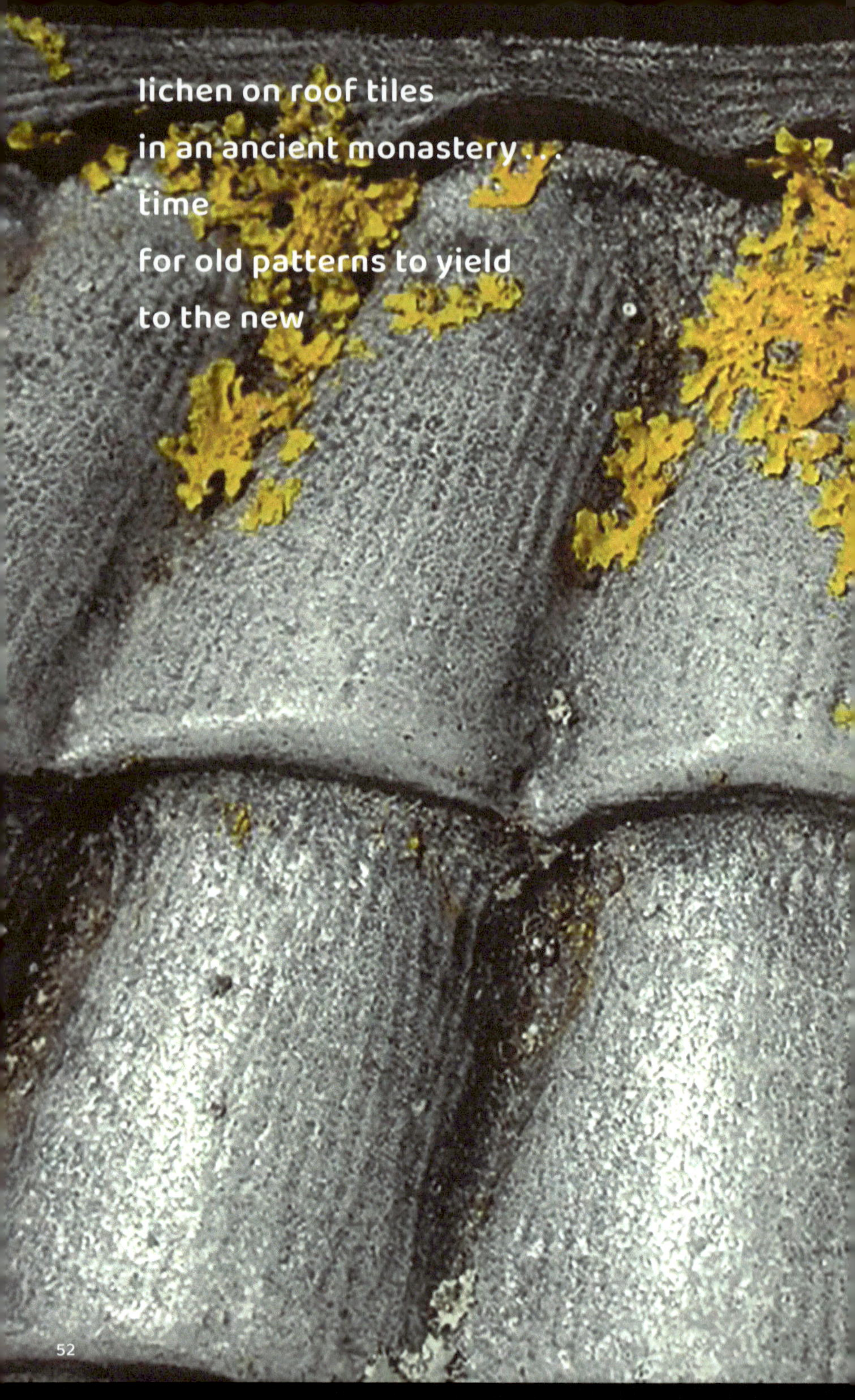

lichen on roof tiles
in an ancient monastery . . .
time
for old patterns to yield
to the new

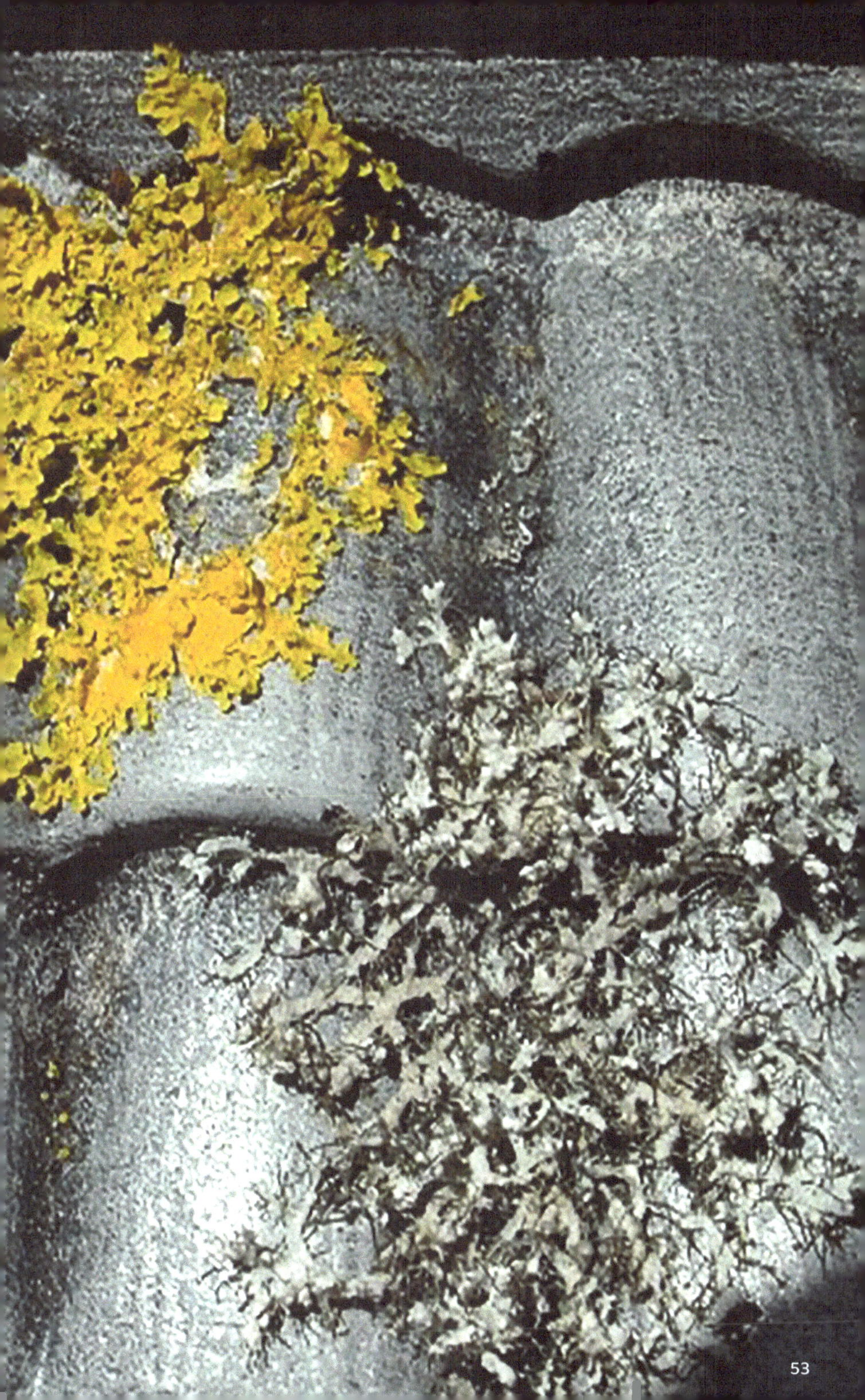

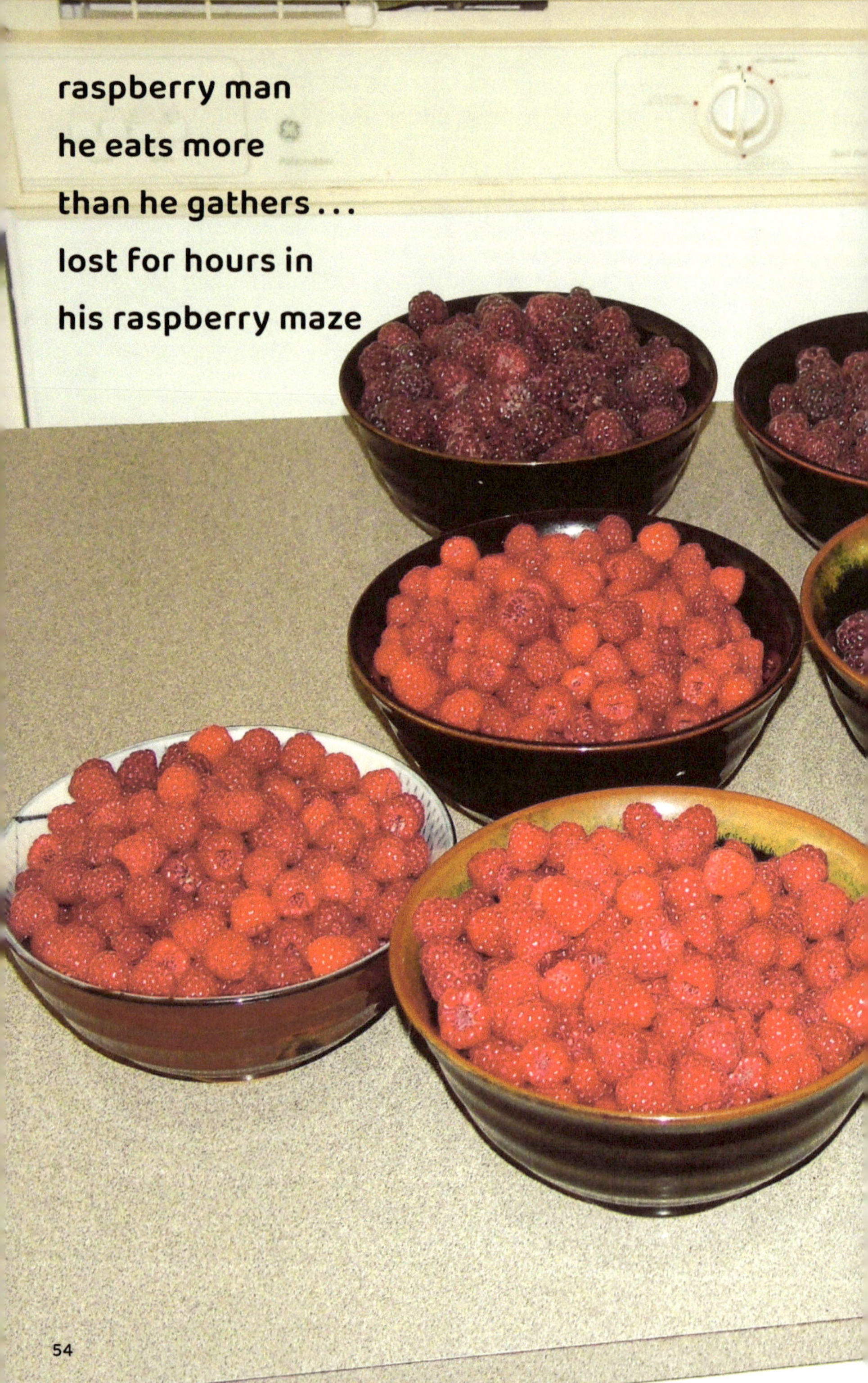

raspberry man
he eats more
than he gathers . . .
lost for hours in
his raspberry maze

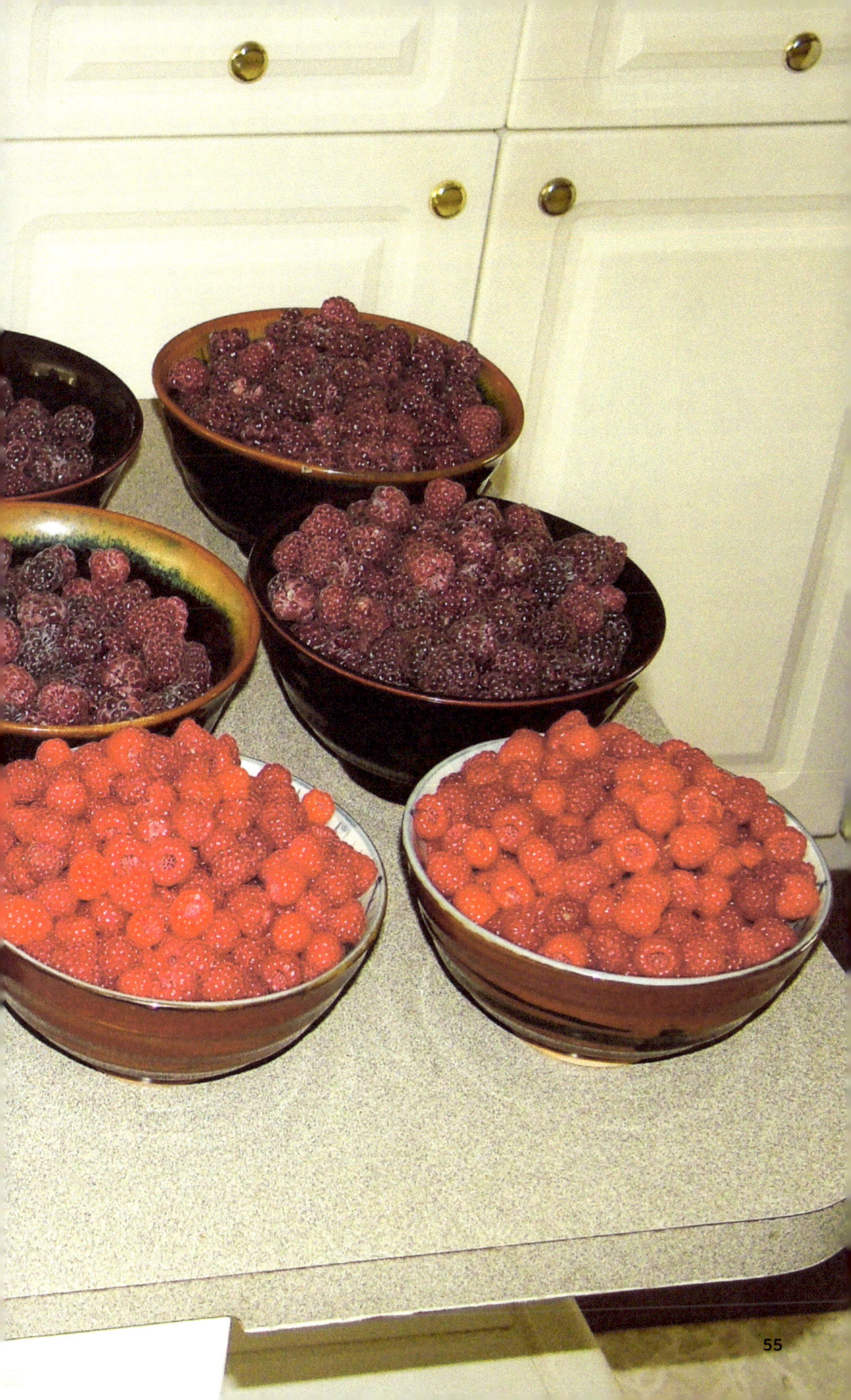

living on an island
the ferry looms large . . .
is it moving off,
or is it waiting
for an ambulance?

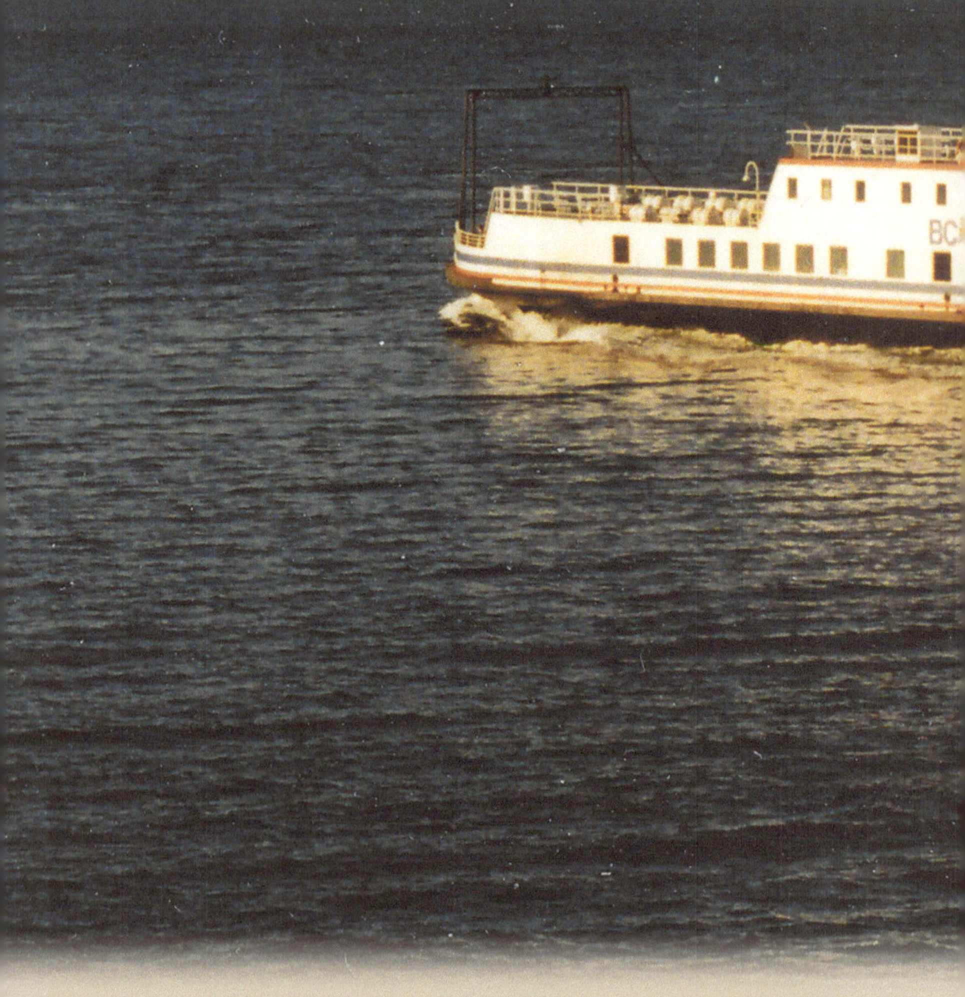

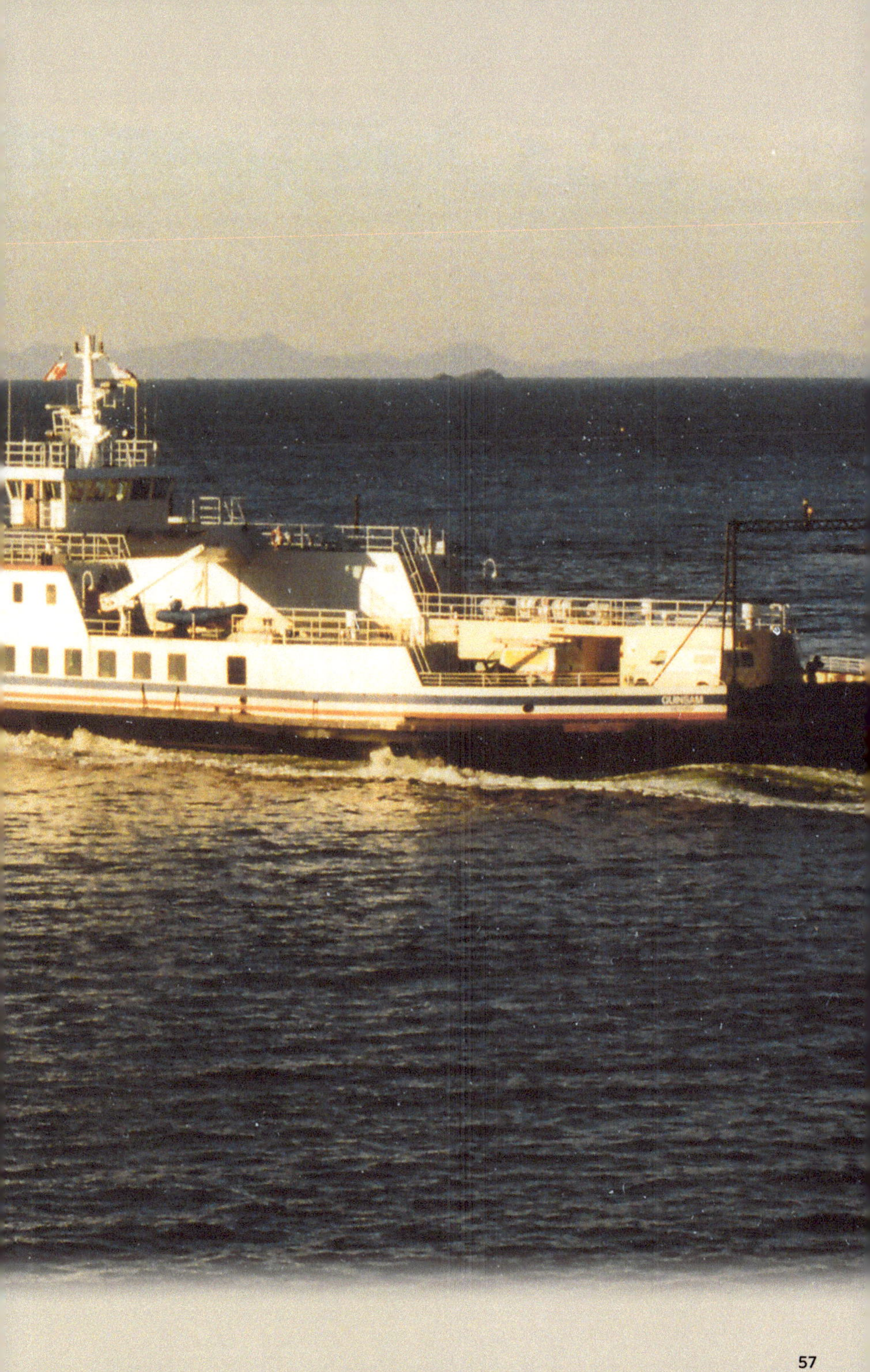

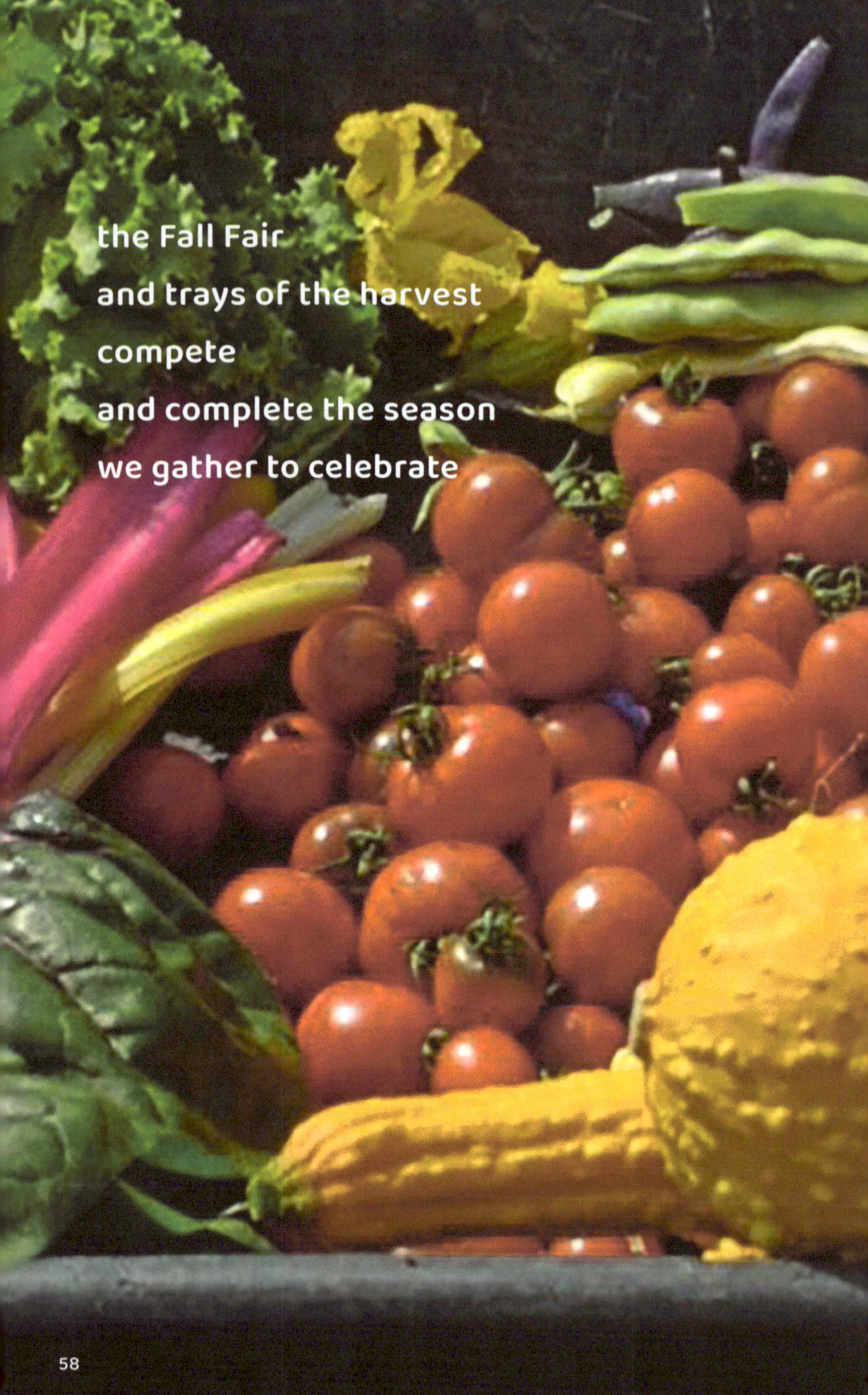

the Fall Fair
and trays of the harvest
compete
and complete the season
we gather to celebrate

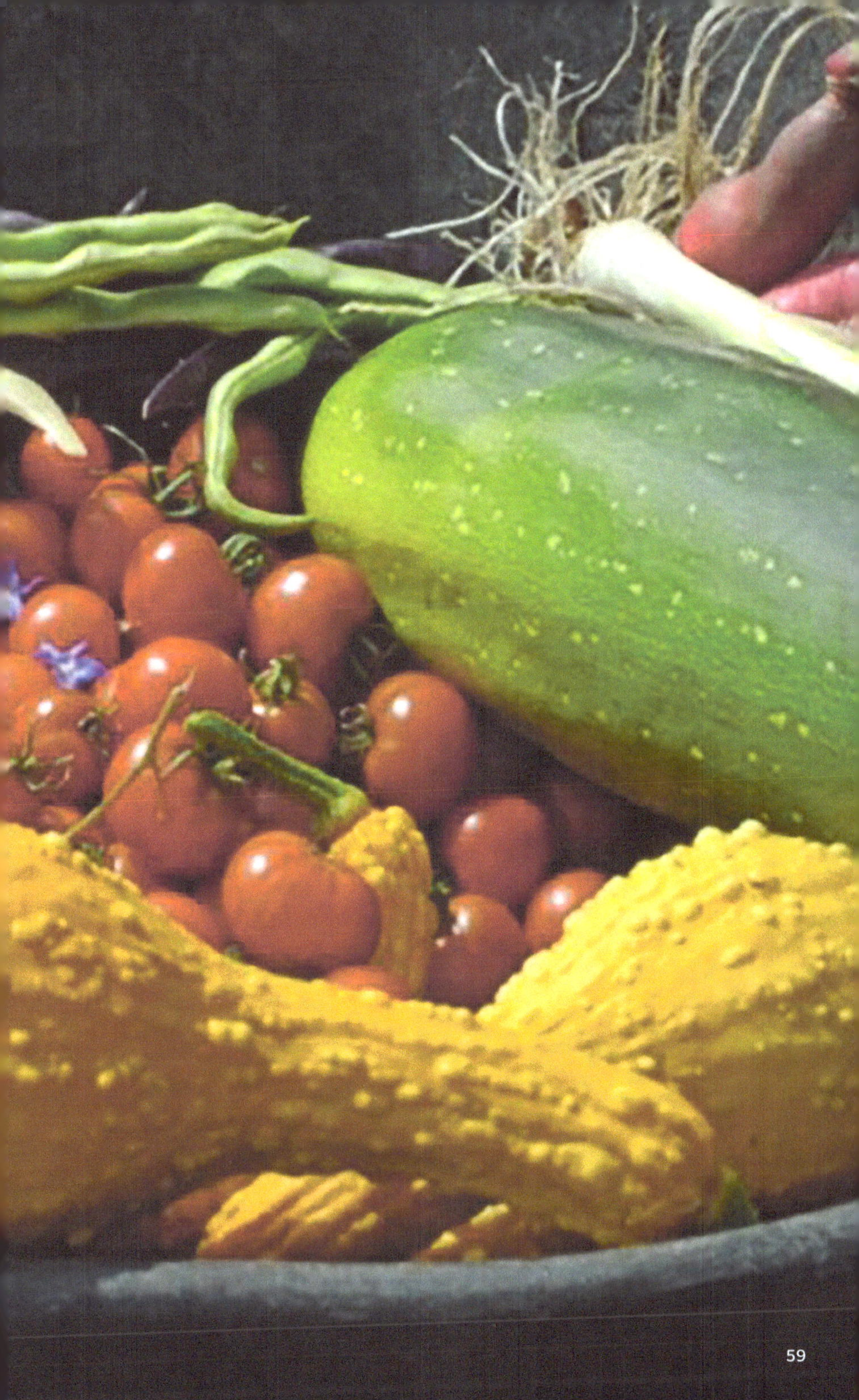

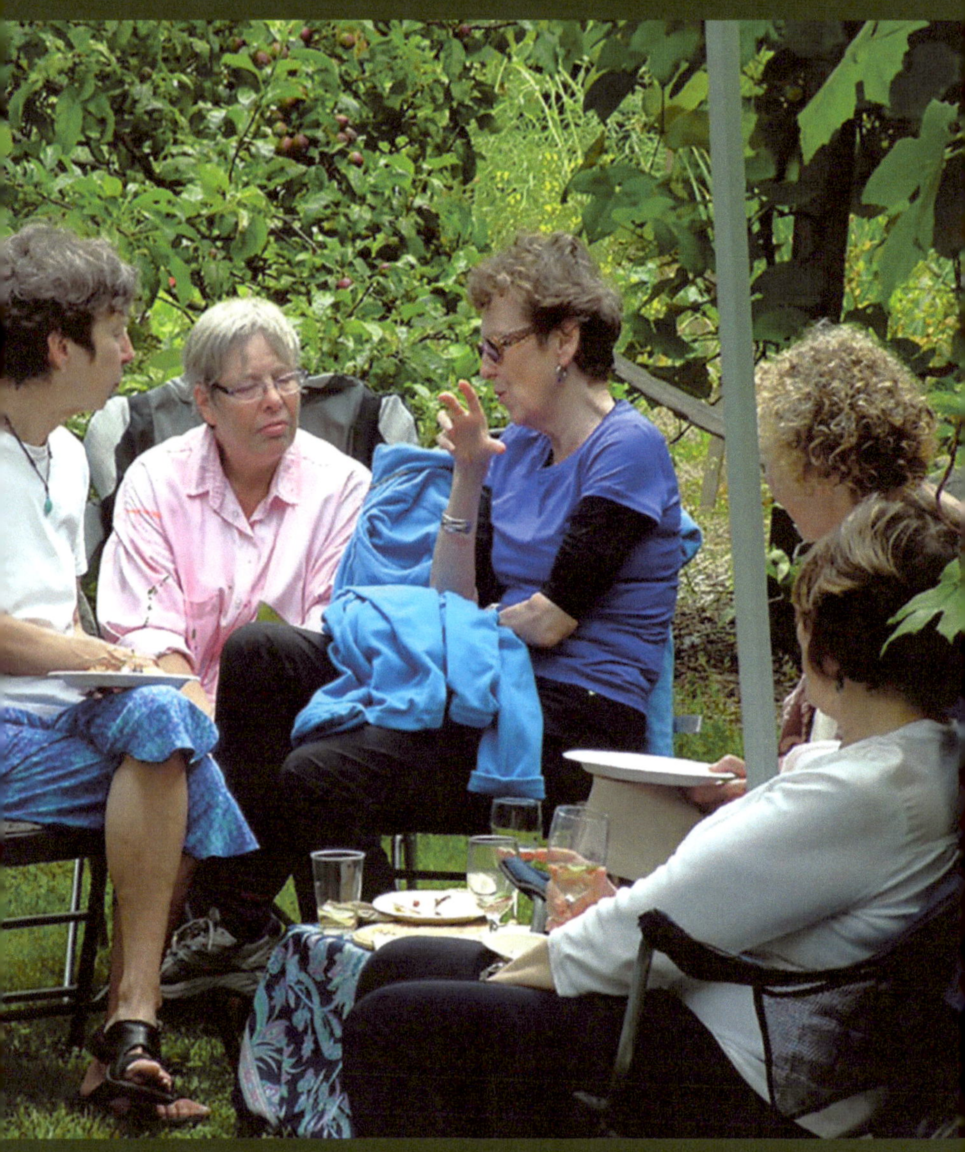

friends enjoying
a long summer afternoon
before
cool winds from the beach
prelude the coming of Fall

he swam

all year round . . .

gaining praise

from passing Gabriolans

and astonished visitors

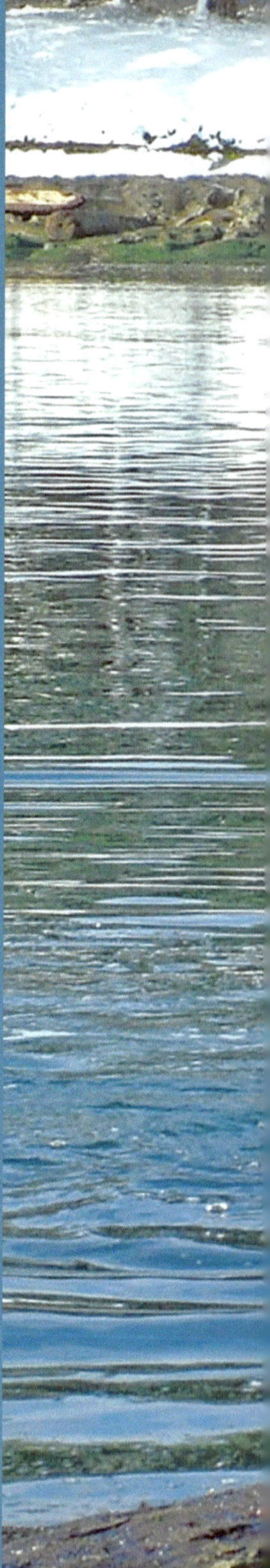

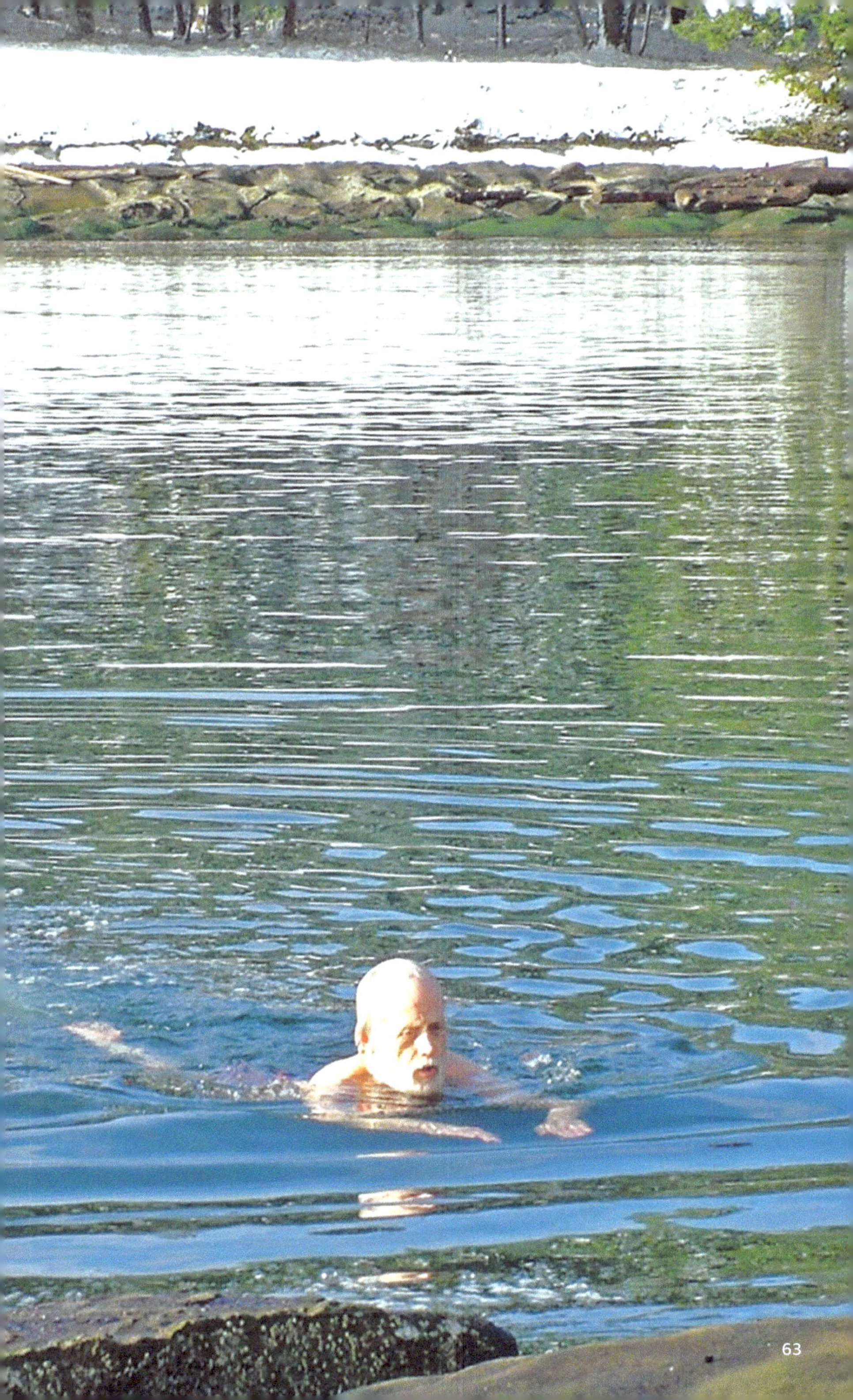

I have always
loved the world
of shadows . . .
less threatening perhaps than
the fierceness of reality

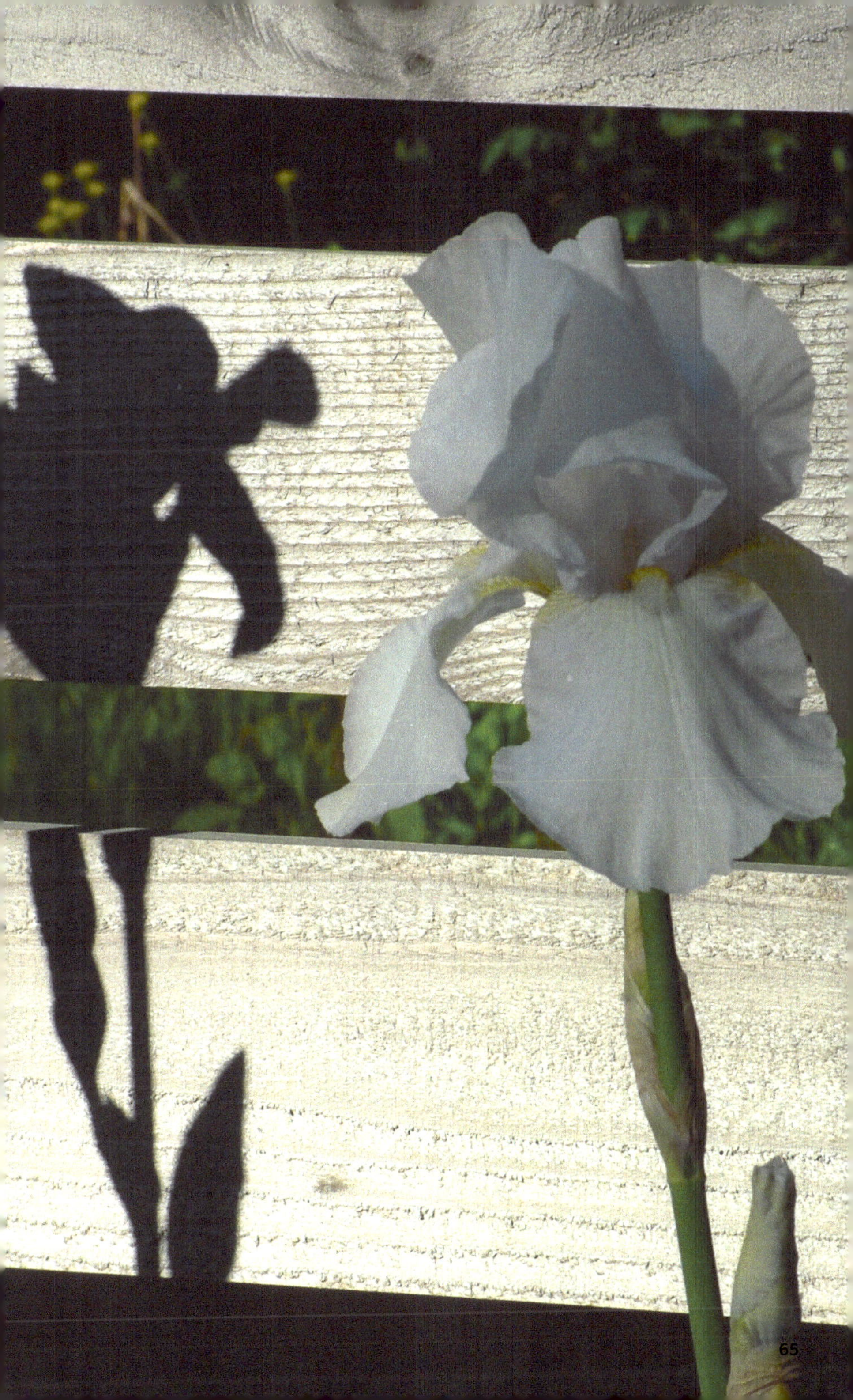

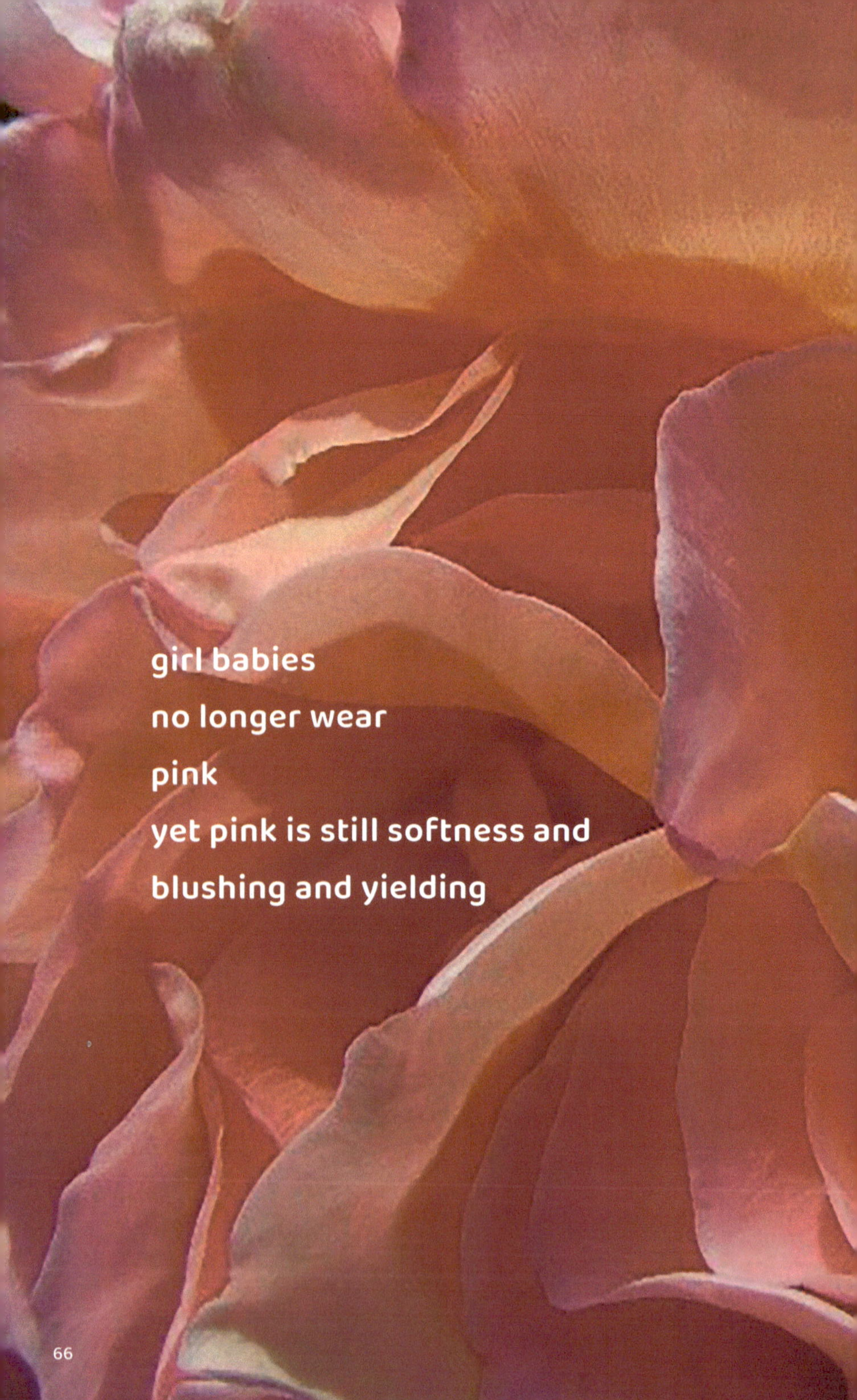

girl babies
no longer wear
pink
yet pink is still softness and
blushing and yielding

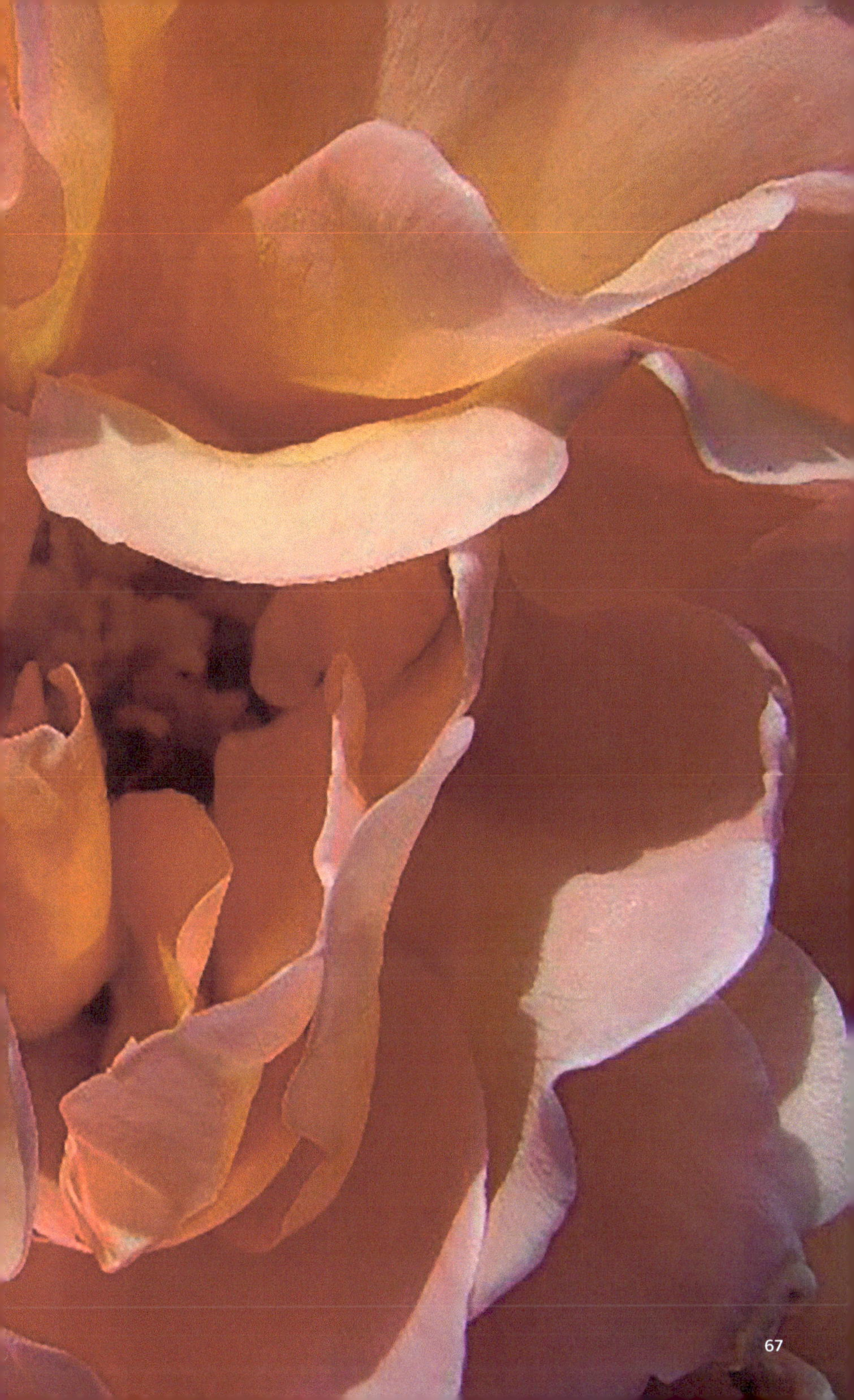

our years in Japan
and yet this irrelevant
image
is one that lingers longest
with me

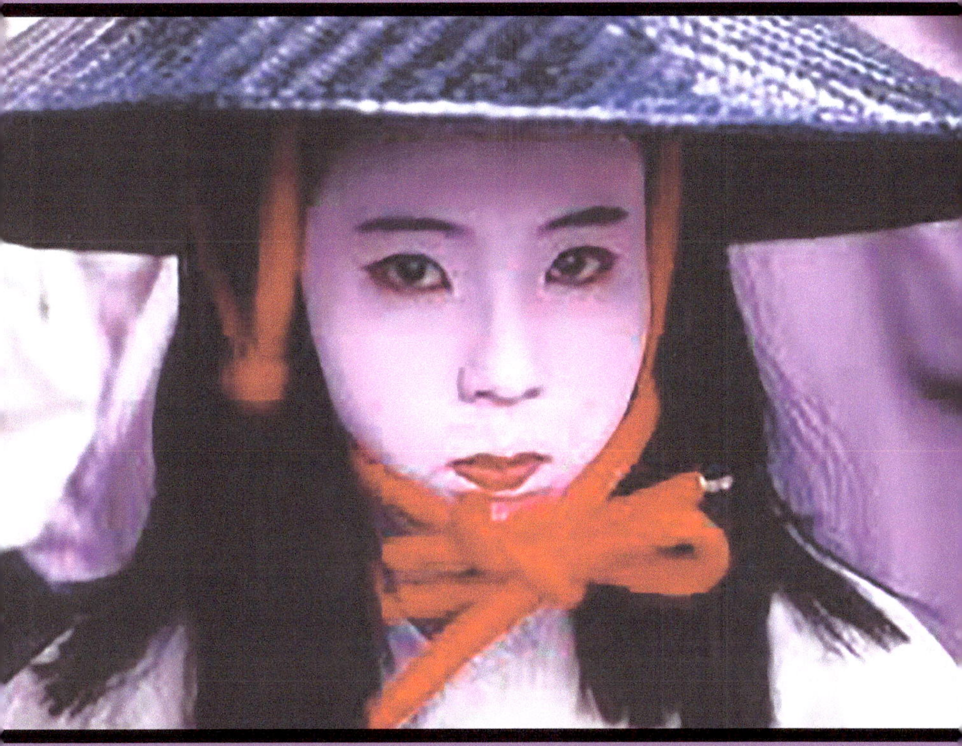

our island

fills its own needs . . .

a bus—now we've a fleet,

a clinic—no problem,

we'll build one for ourselves

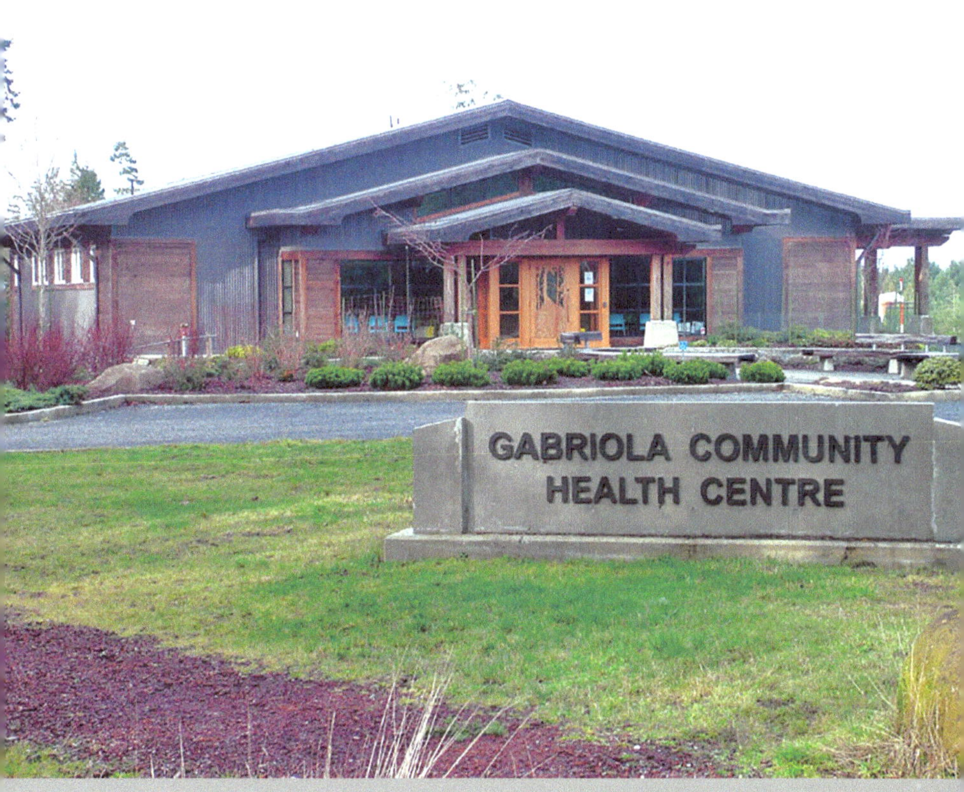
GABRIOLA COMMUNITY
HEALTH CENTRE

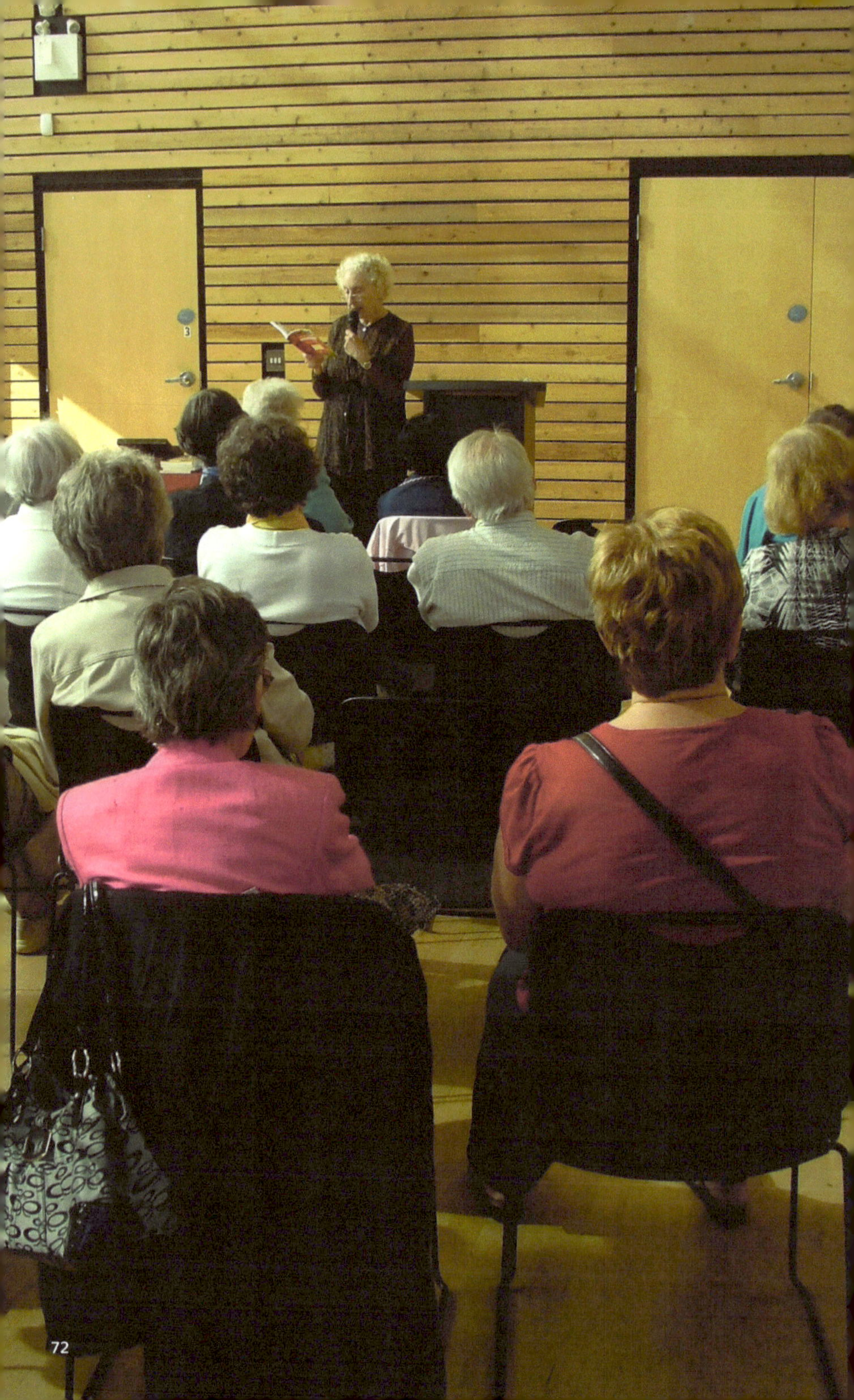

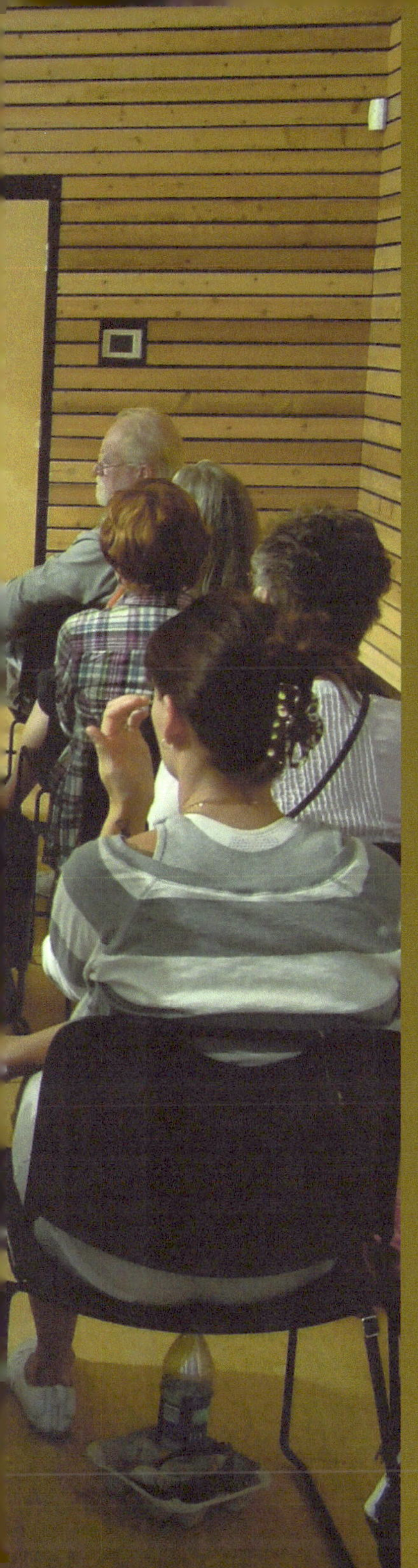

reading

on home ground . . .

their applause

has sustained me

over the years

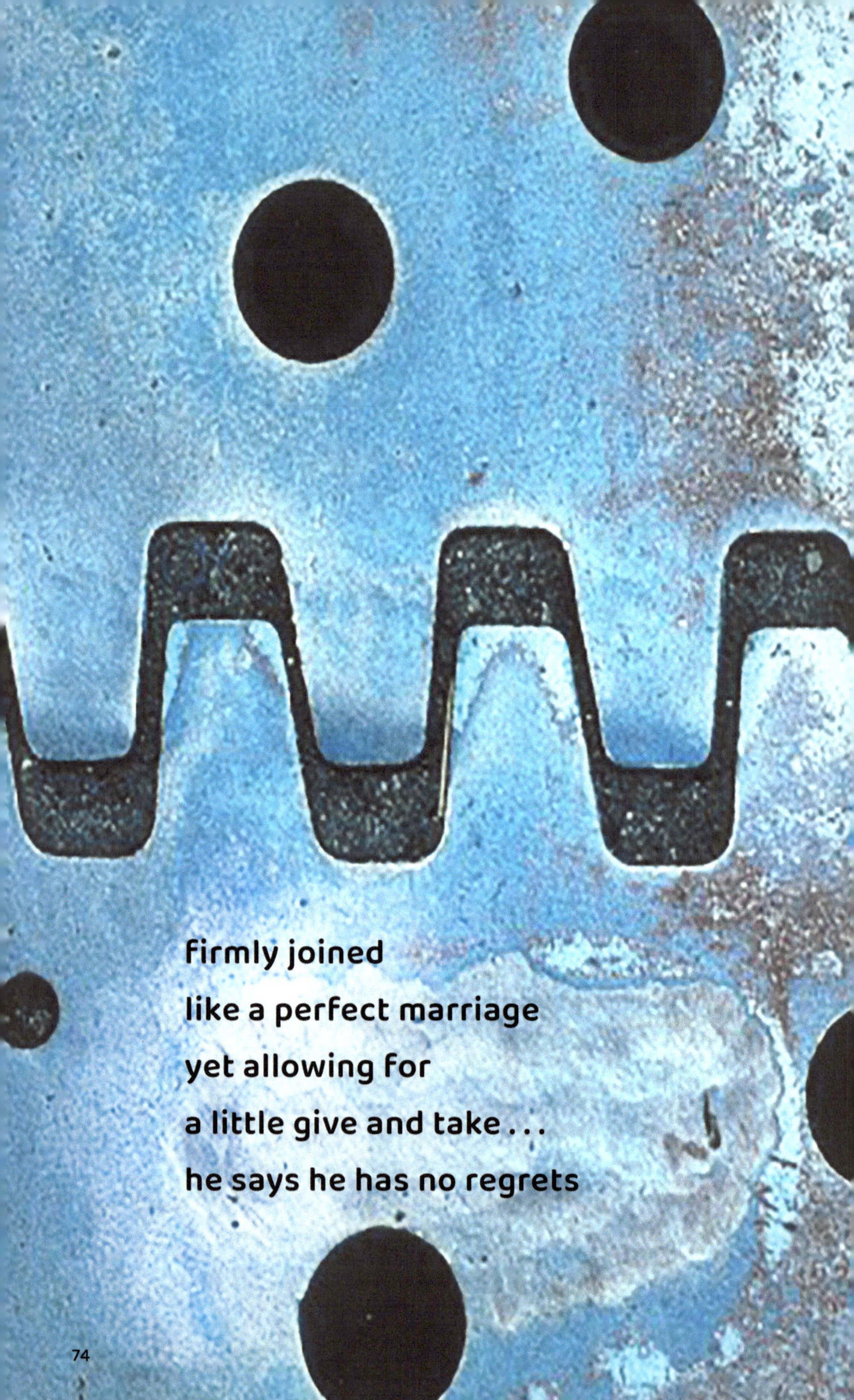

firmly joined
like a perfect marriage
yet allowing for
a little give and take . . .
he says he has no regrets

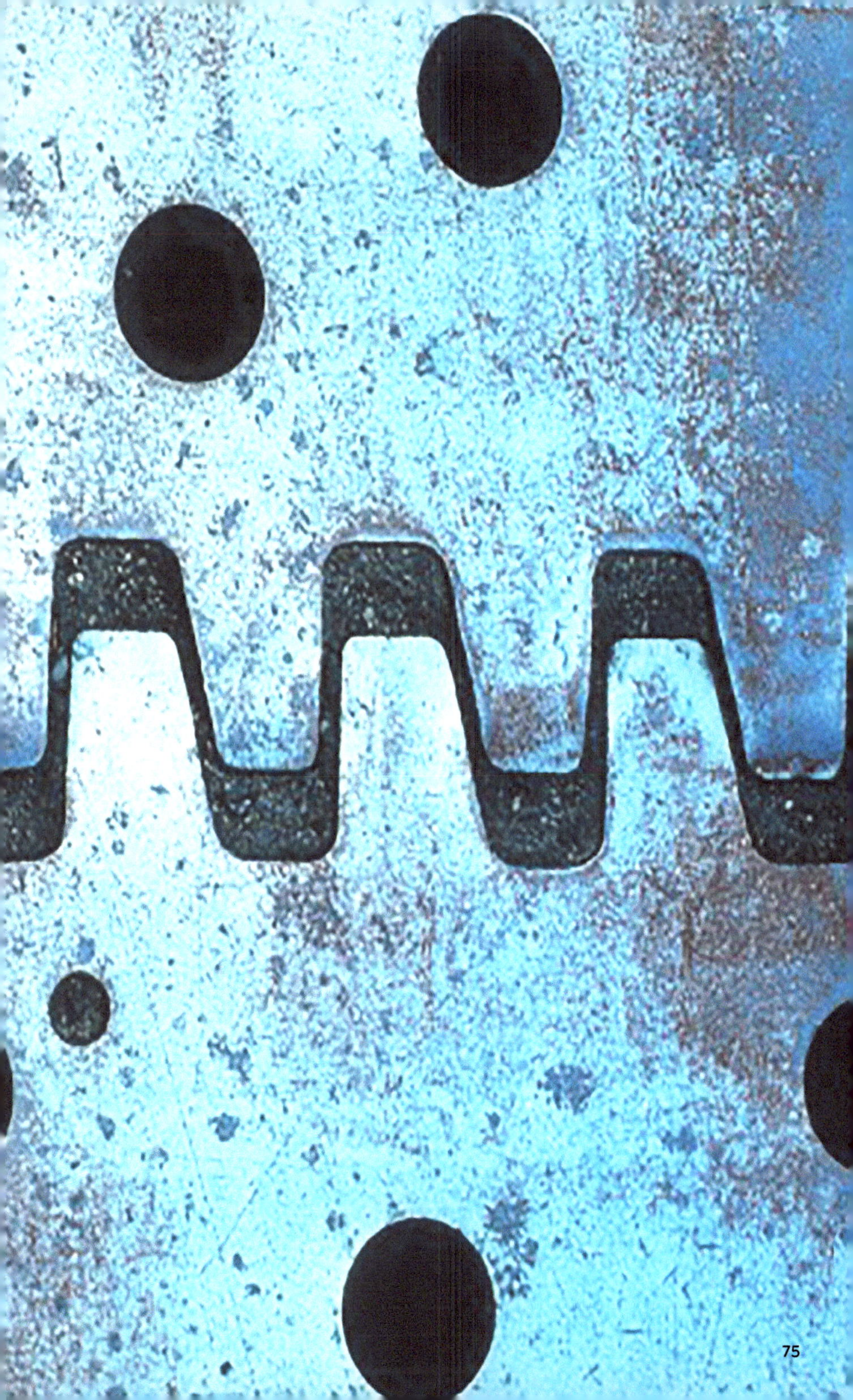

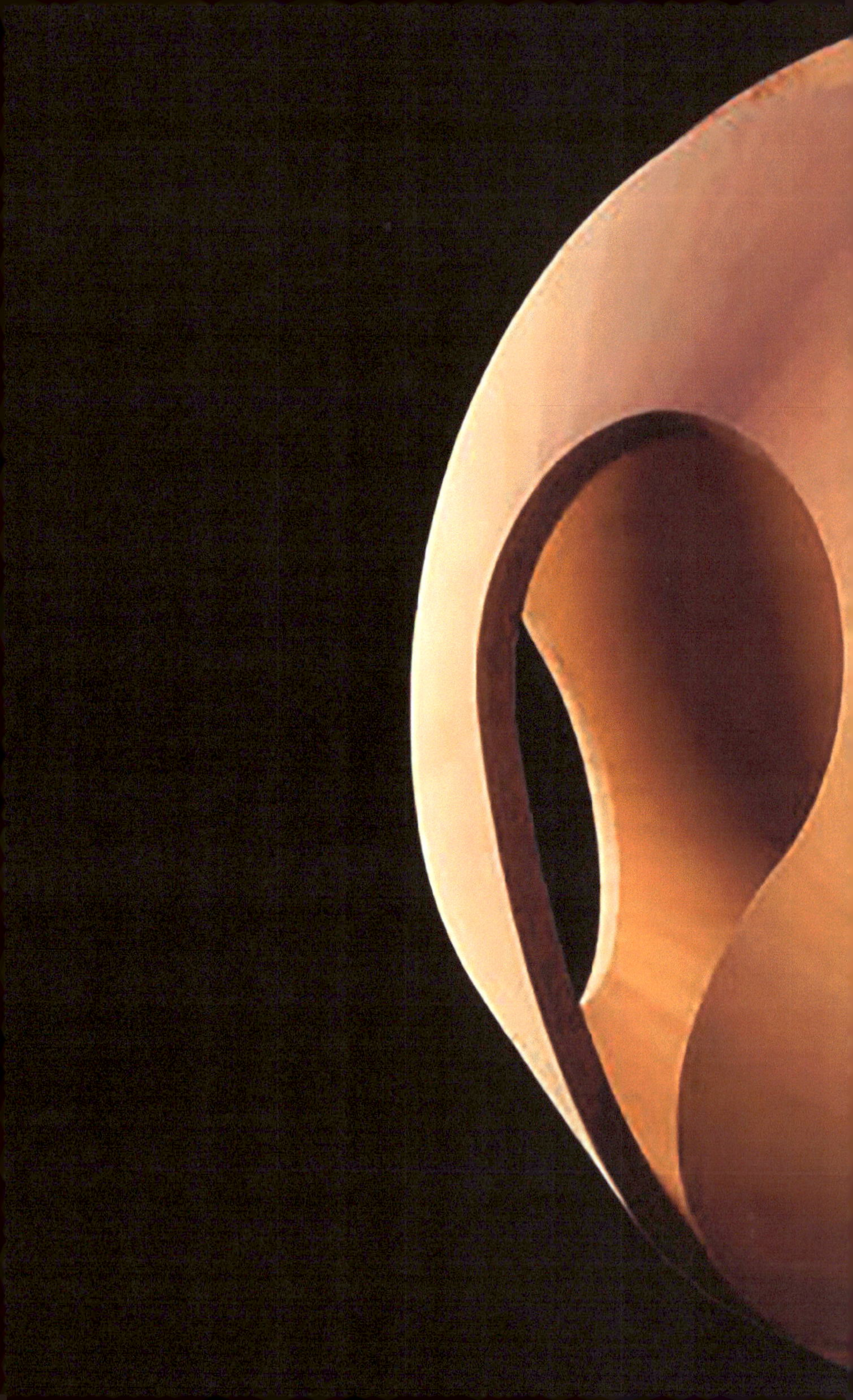

Creativity

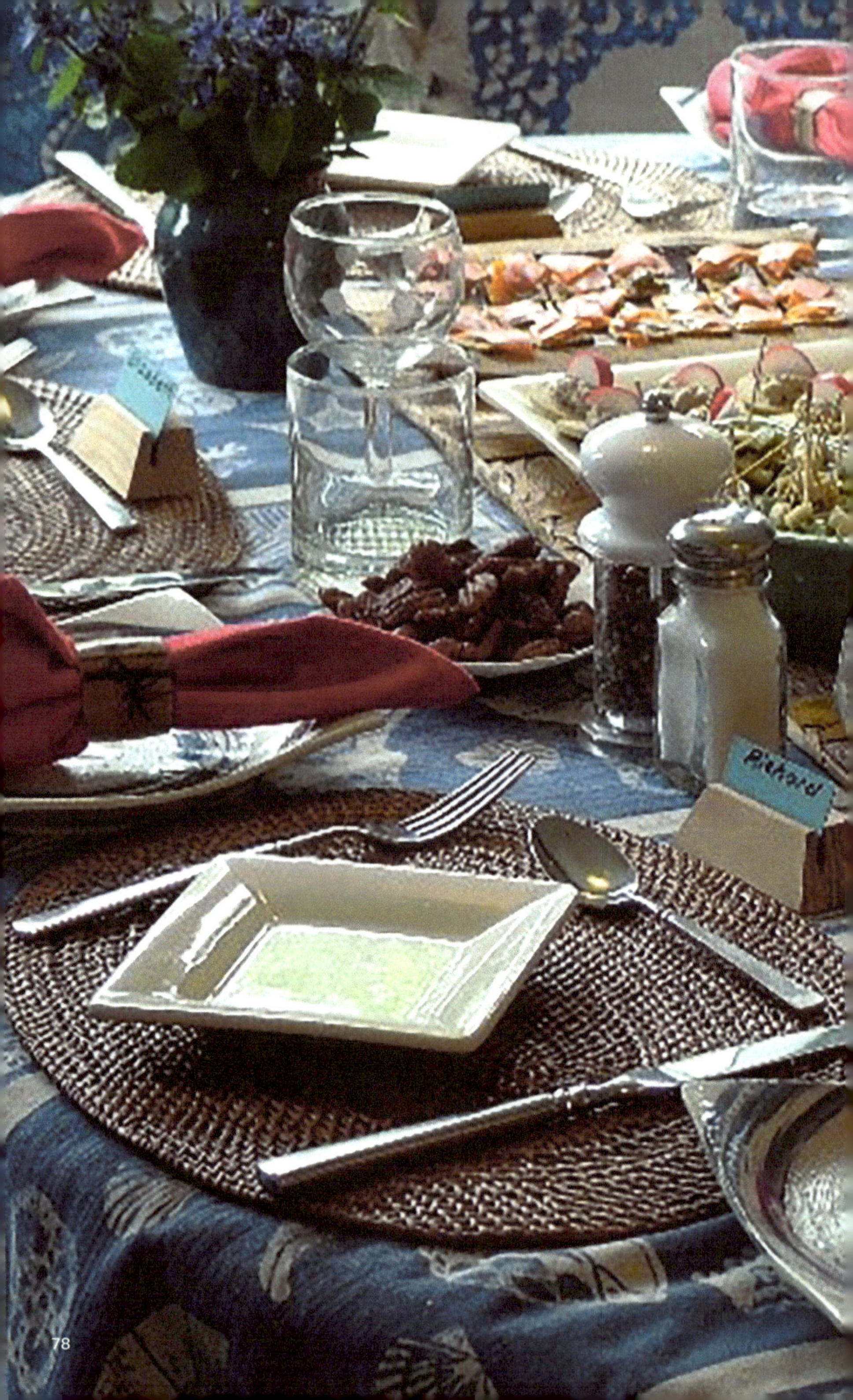
Richard

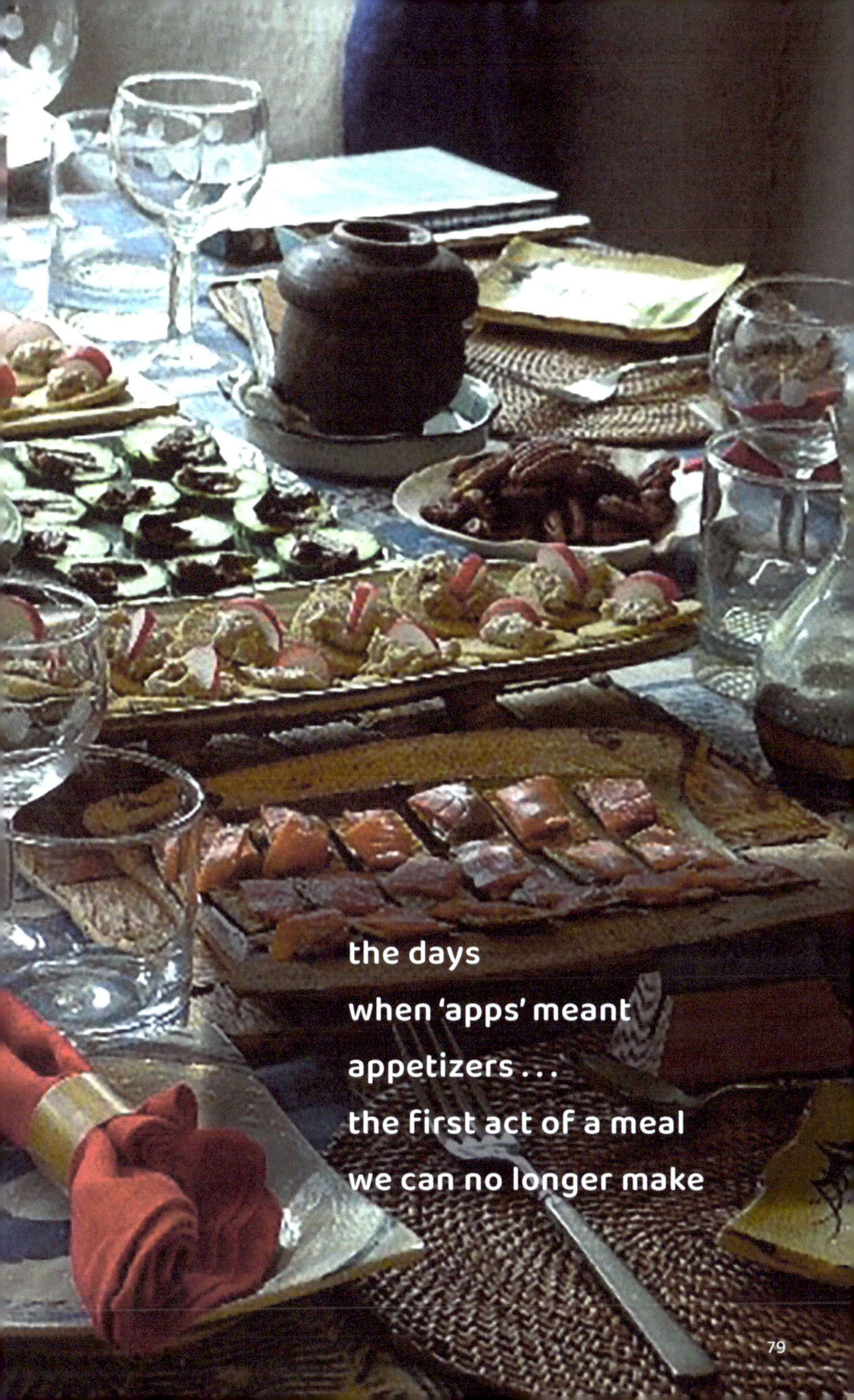

the days
when 'apps' meant
appetizers . . .
the first act of a meal
we can no longer make

perfection
is rare, but when
it occurs
the whole world rejoices
with one full voice

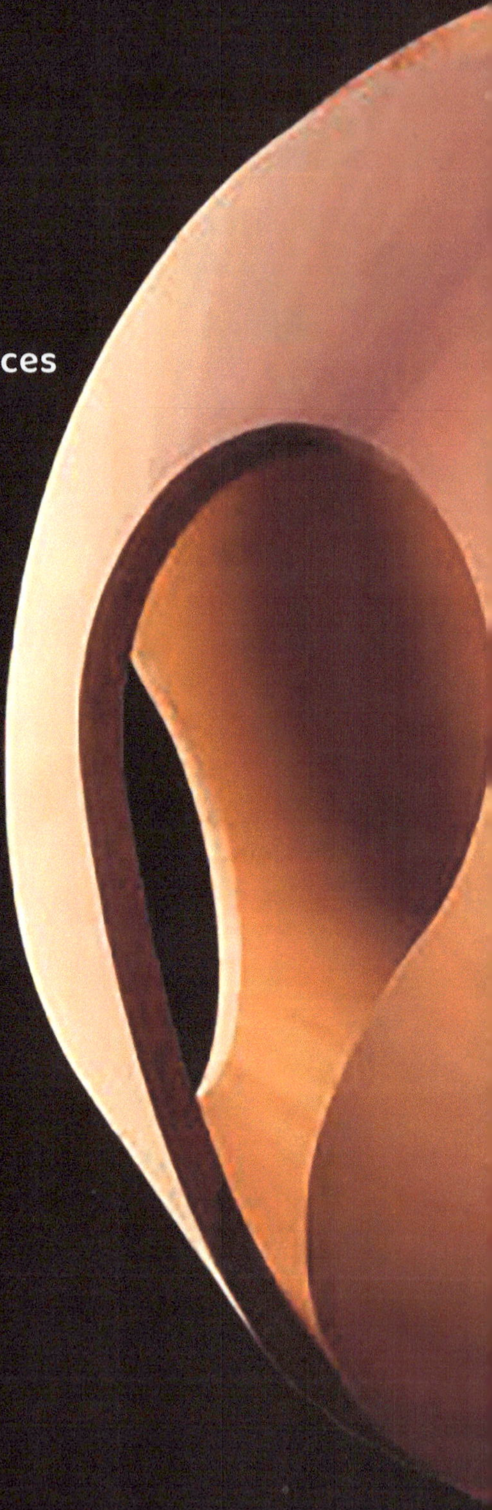

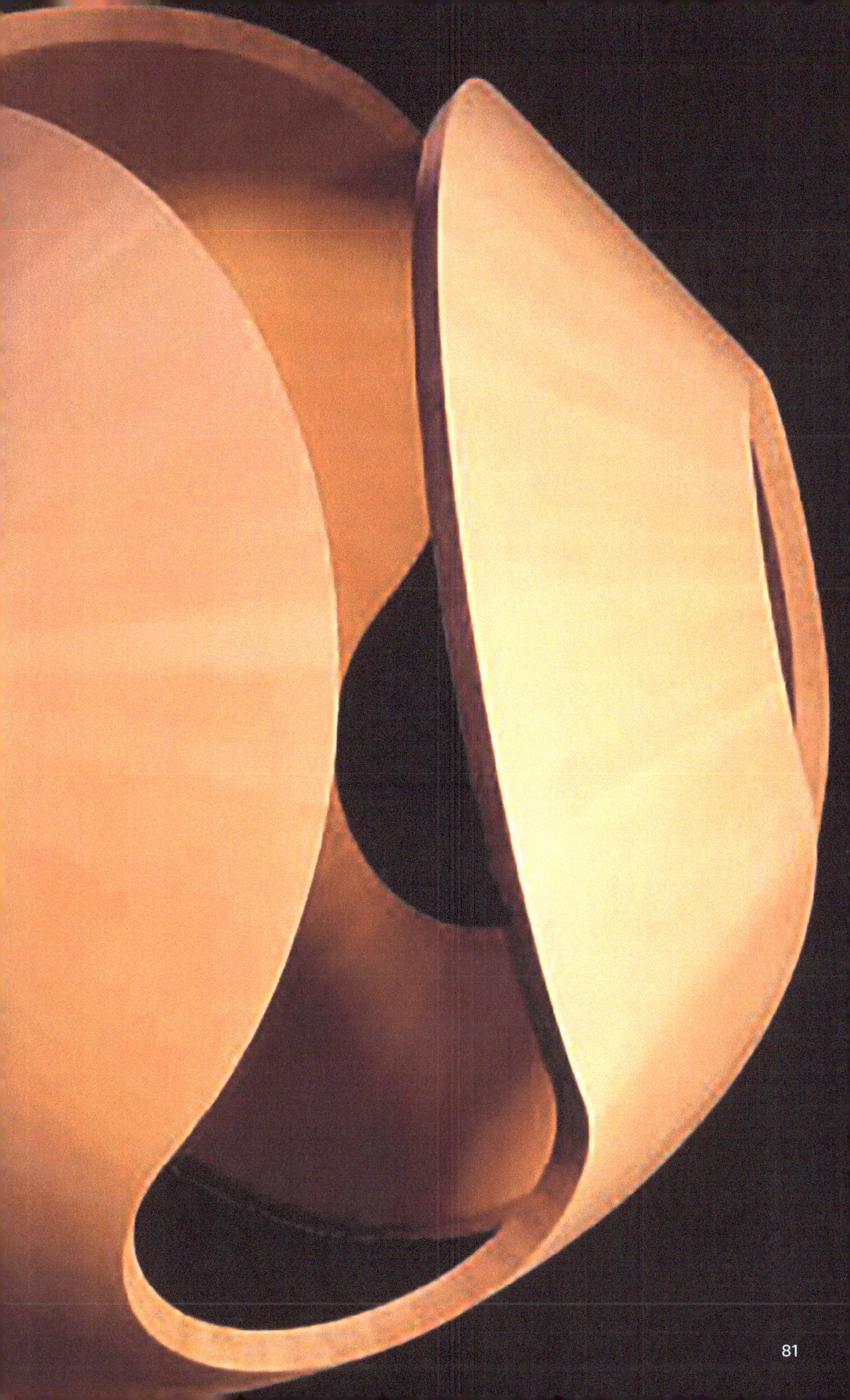

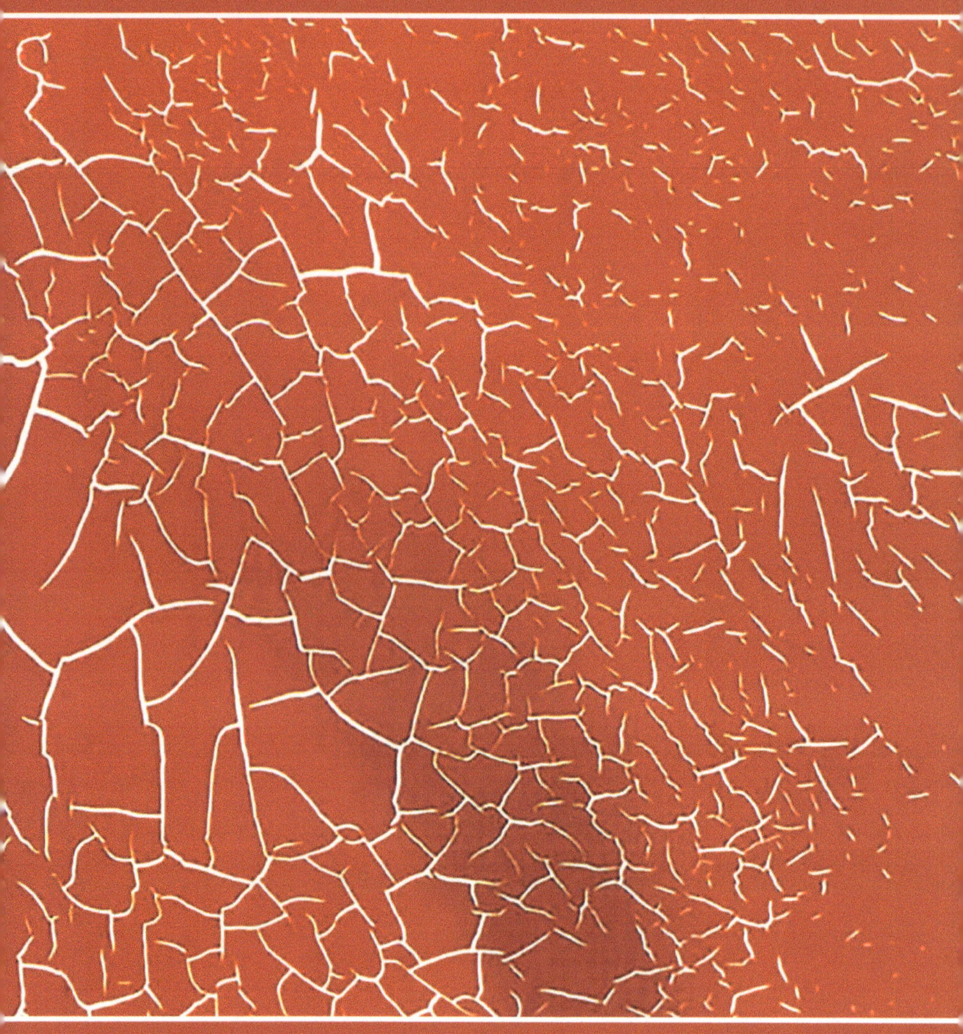

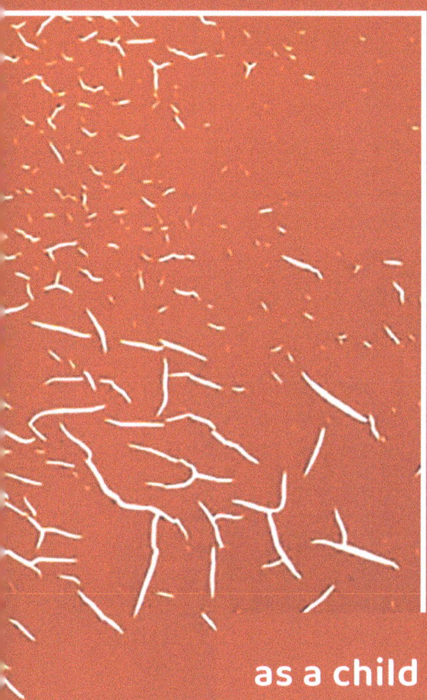

as a child
I could see faces
in the ceiling cracks . . .
now, remembering those times,
flaws in car paint still enthrall

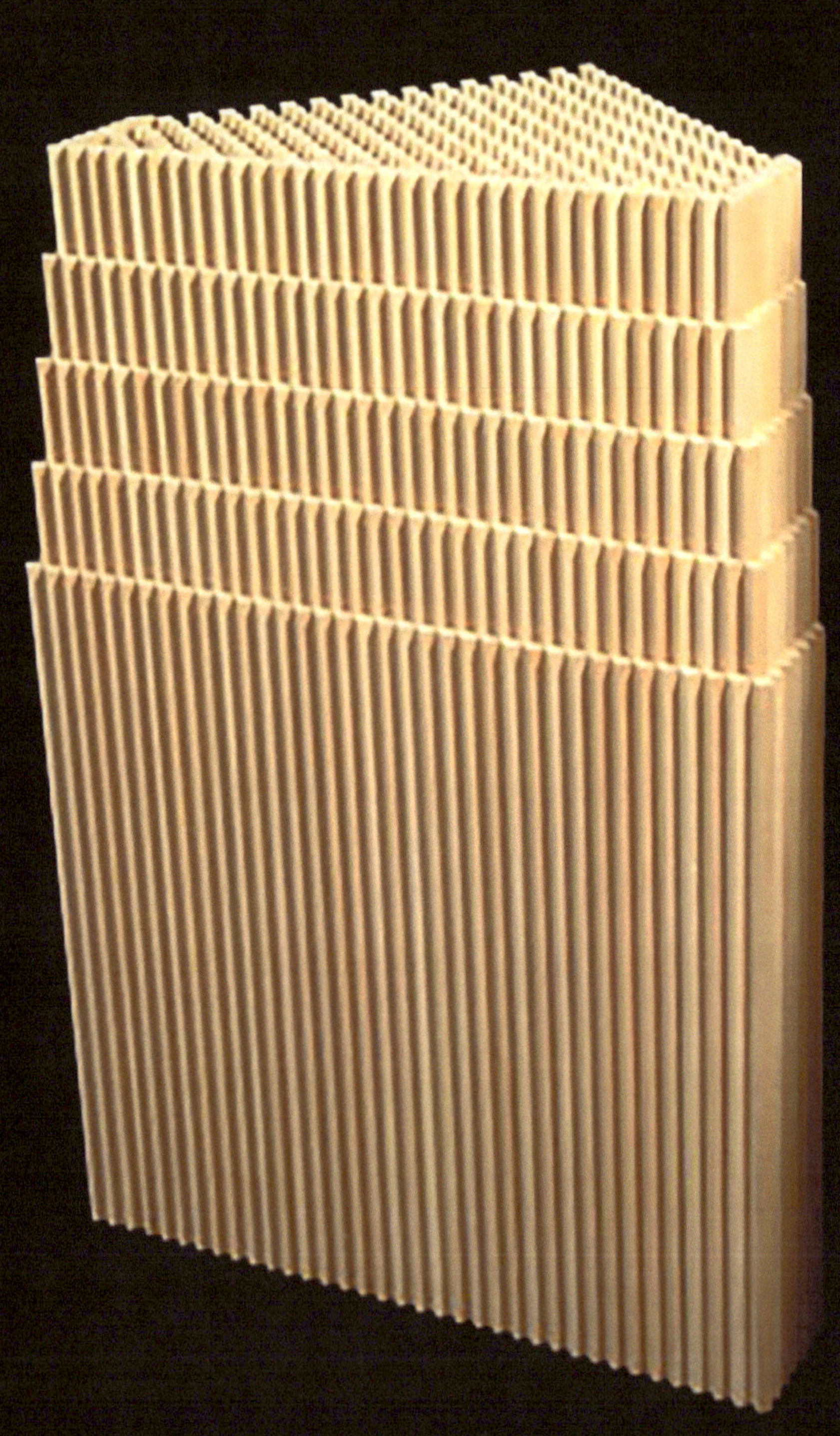

a stick of wood
is not much
on its own . . .
but with a thousand others
it makes the headlines

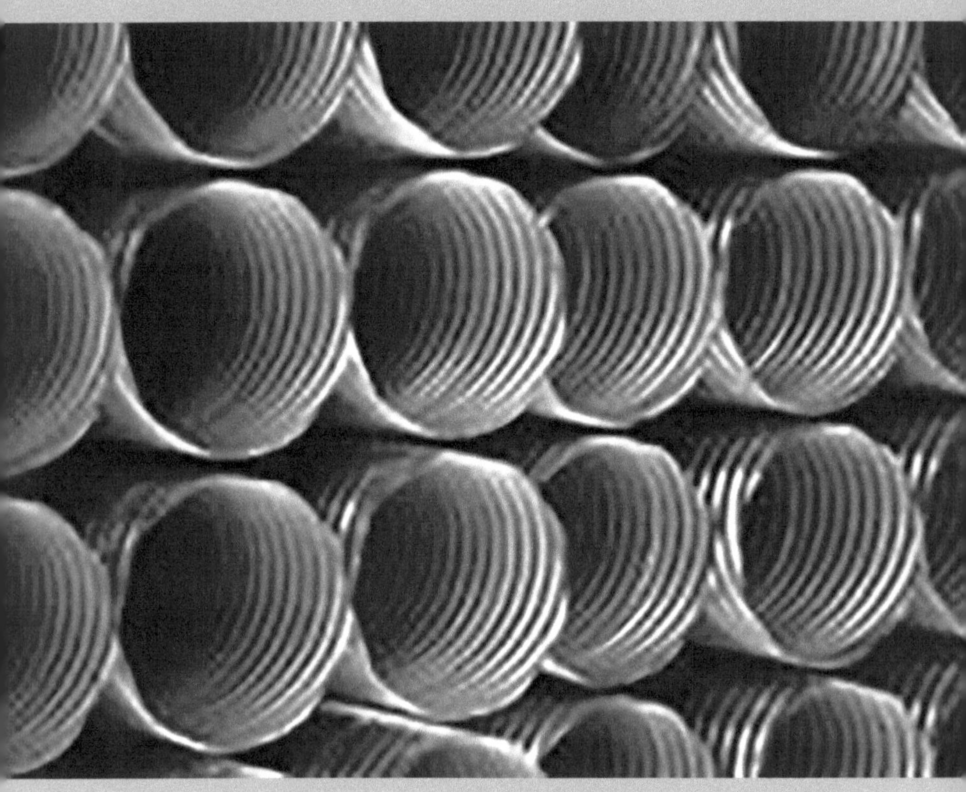

oh!
the roundness of
round things . . .
even these culvert pipes
invite me to curl up round

knitting's
a metaphor for life . . .
the purls and plains
are the ups and downs
before the casting off

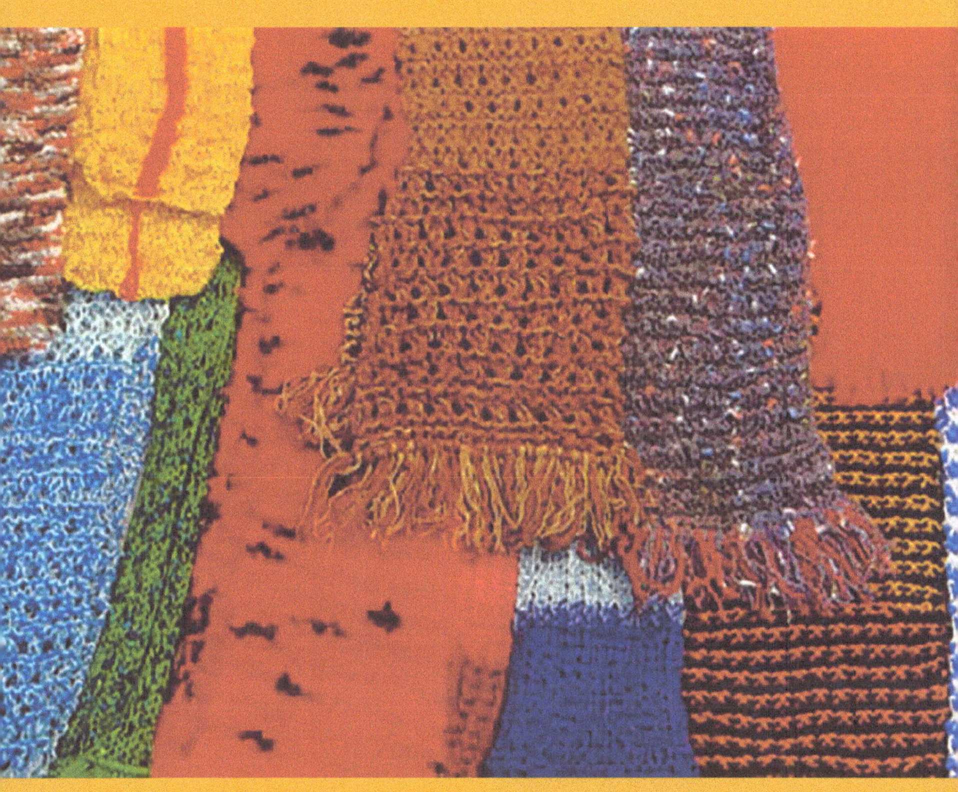

an enso
happens when
the mind is free
so the body can
do its own thing

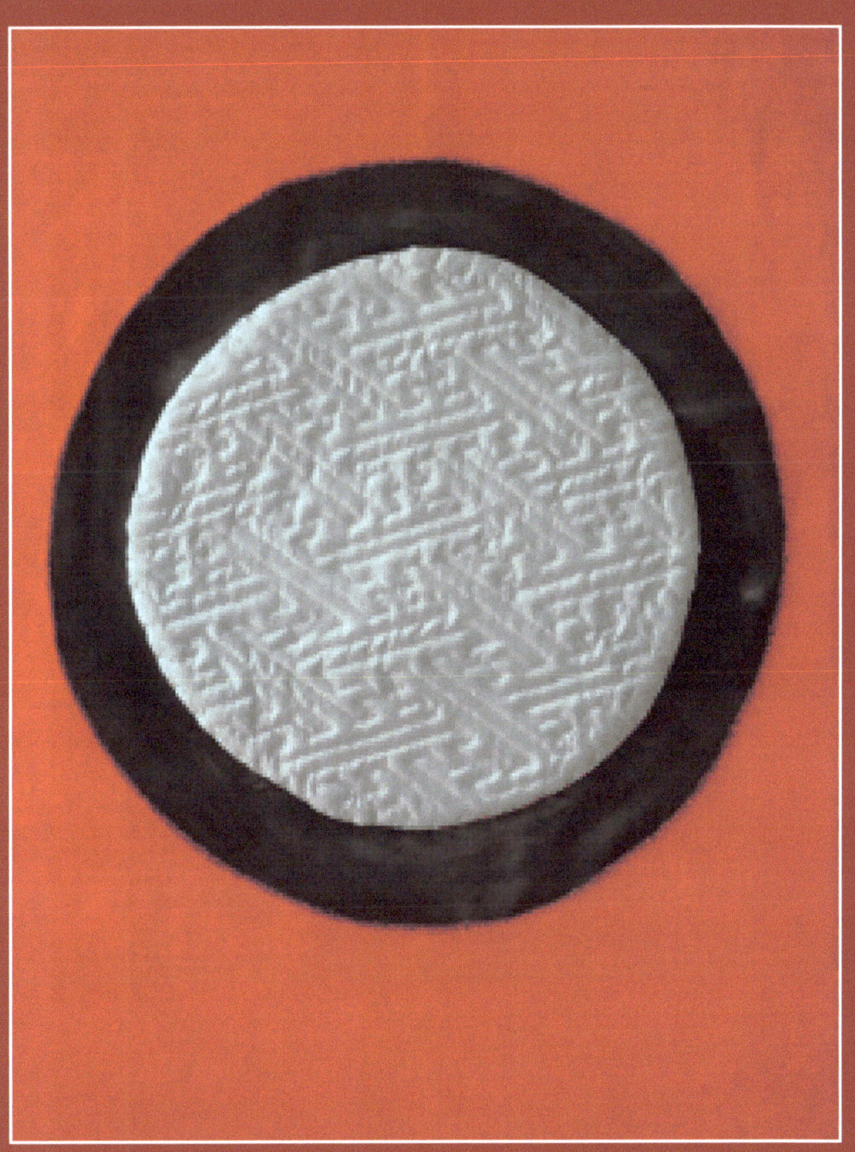

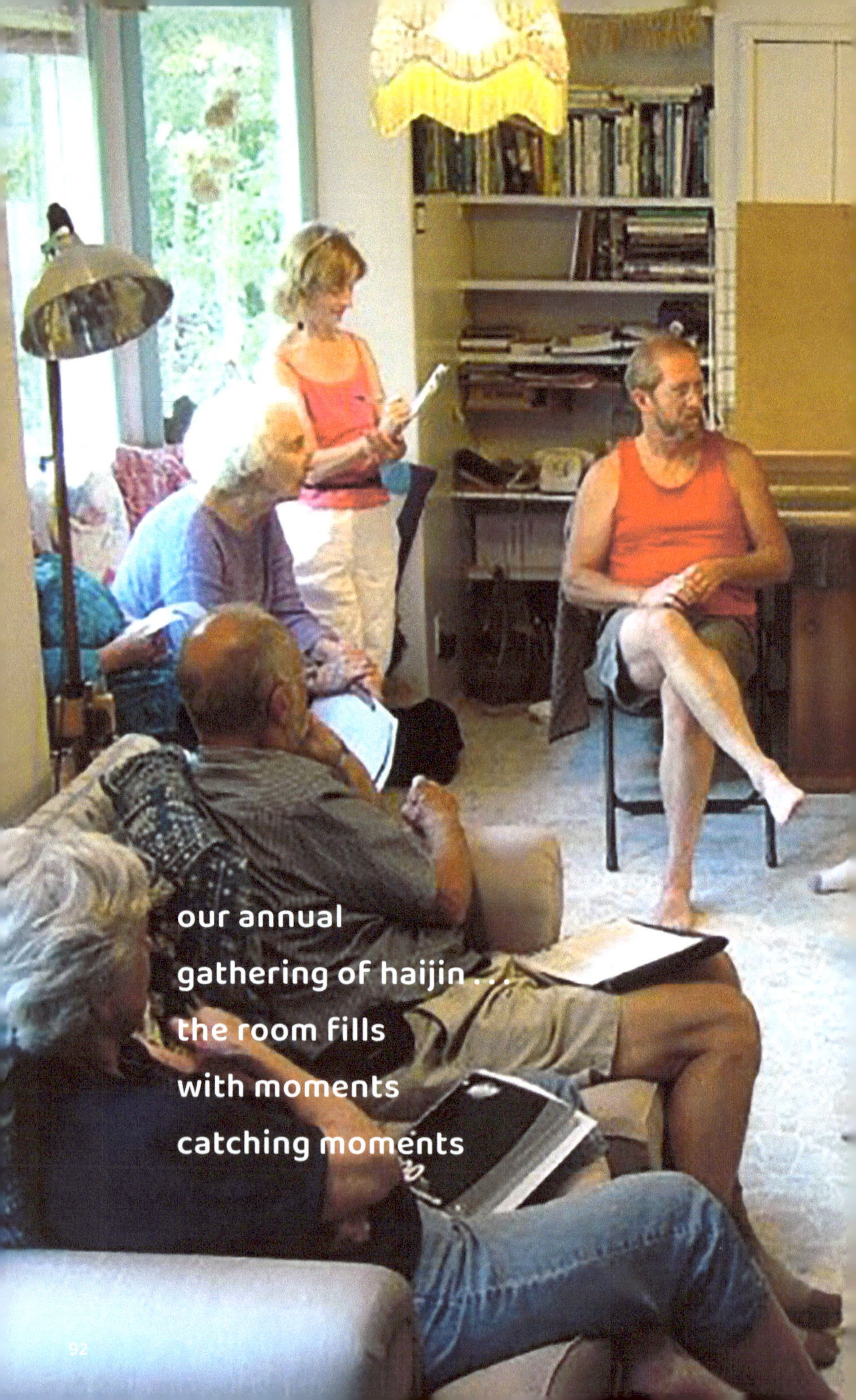

our annual
gathering of haijin . . .
the room fills
with moments
catching moments

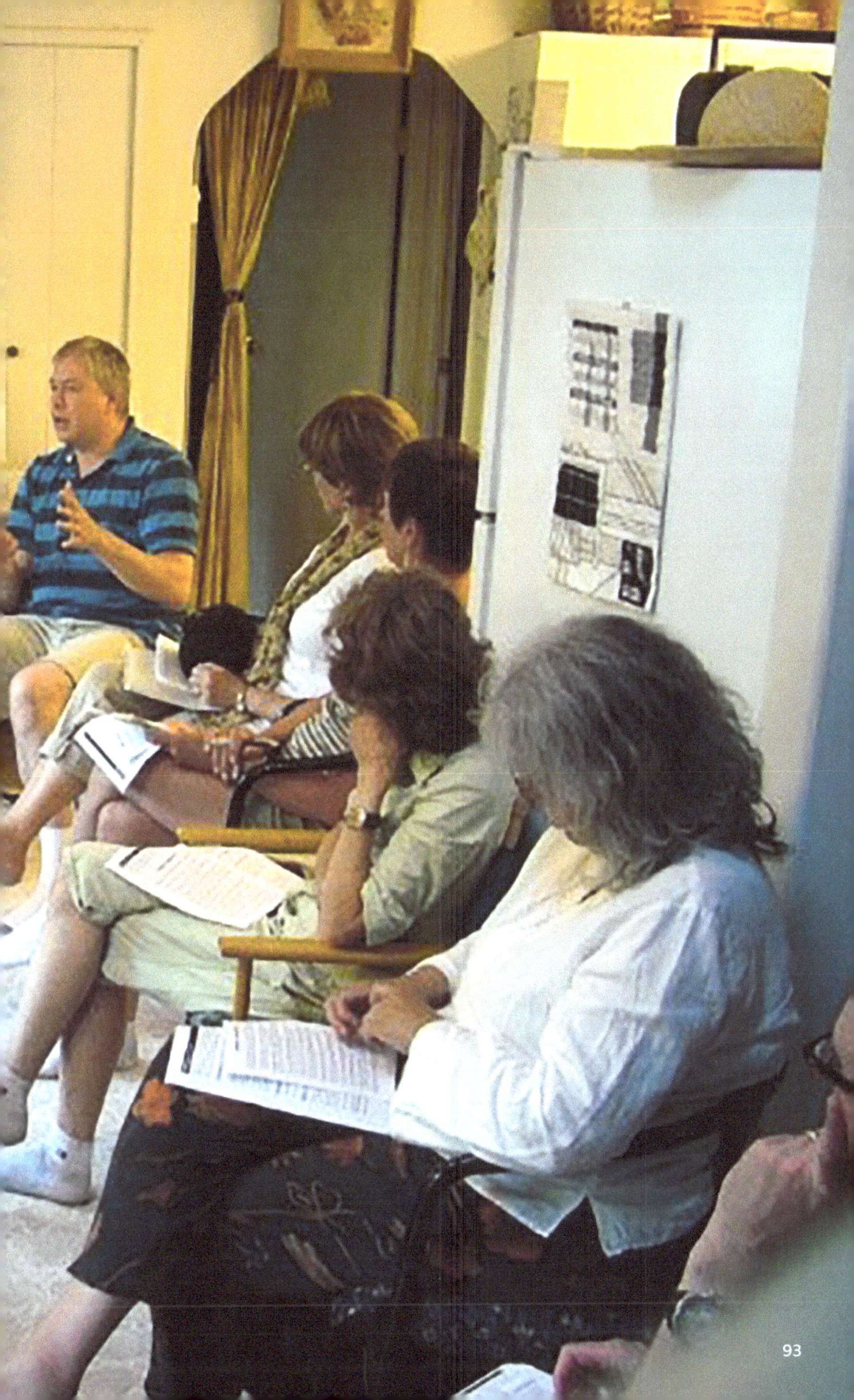

he and I

both know

that

large things come

from piecing small

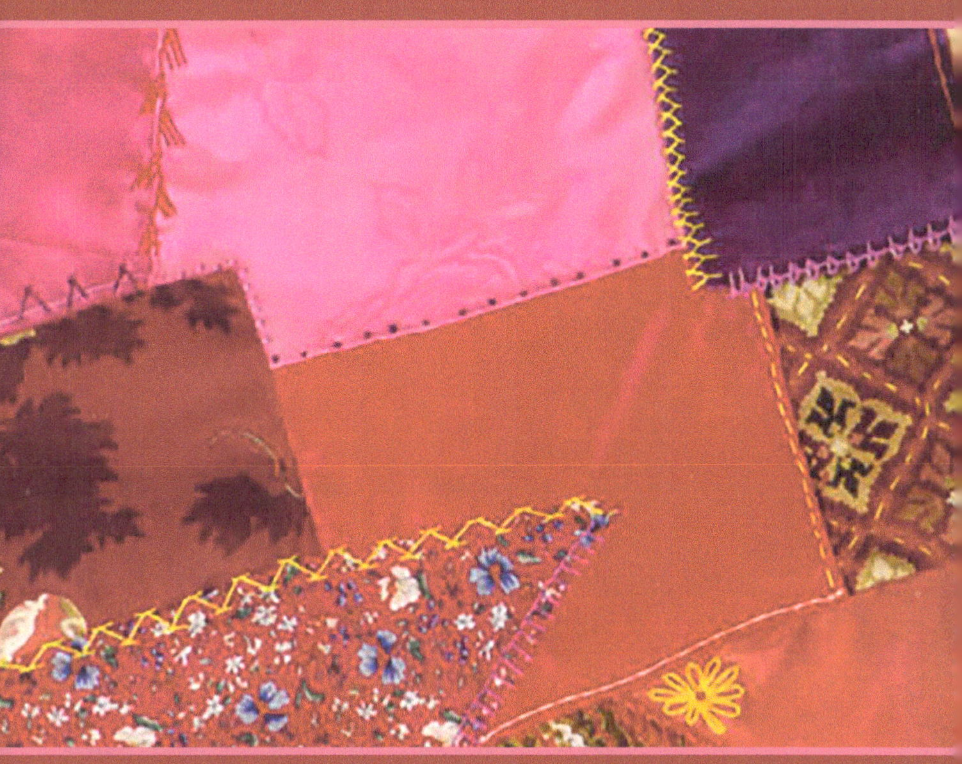

how his world grows
as piece by piece
he assembles
small data into
Big Data

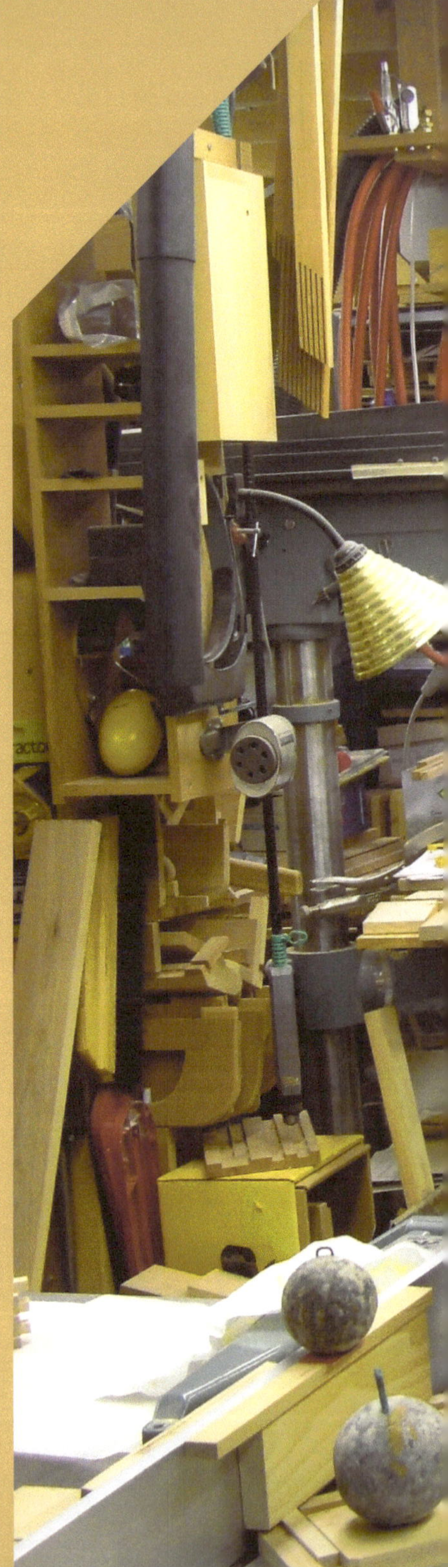

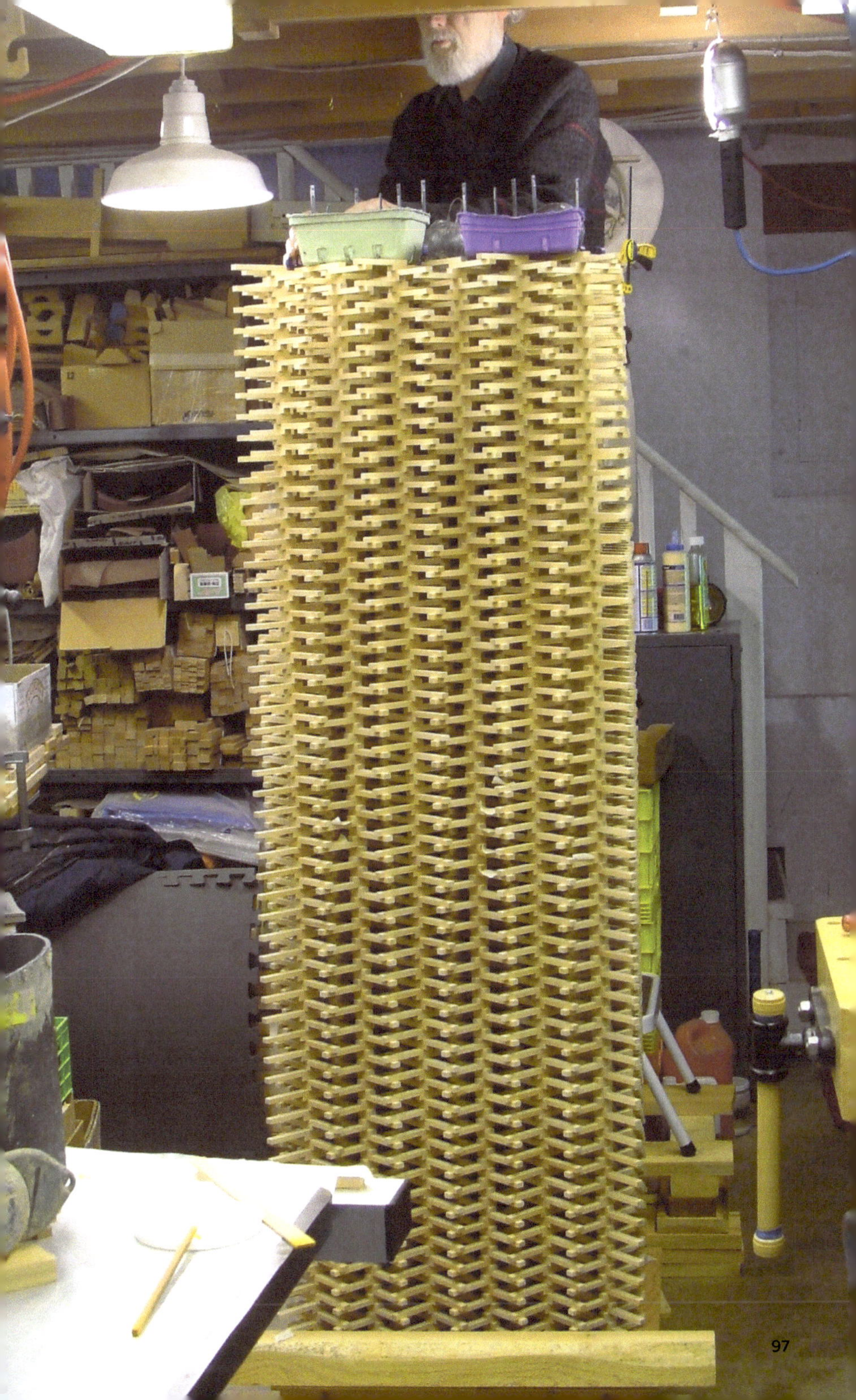

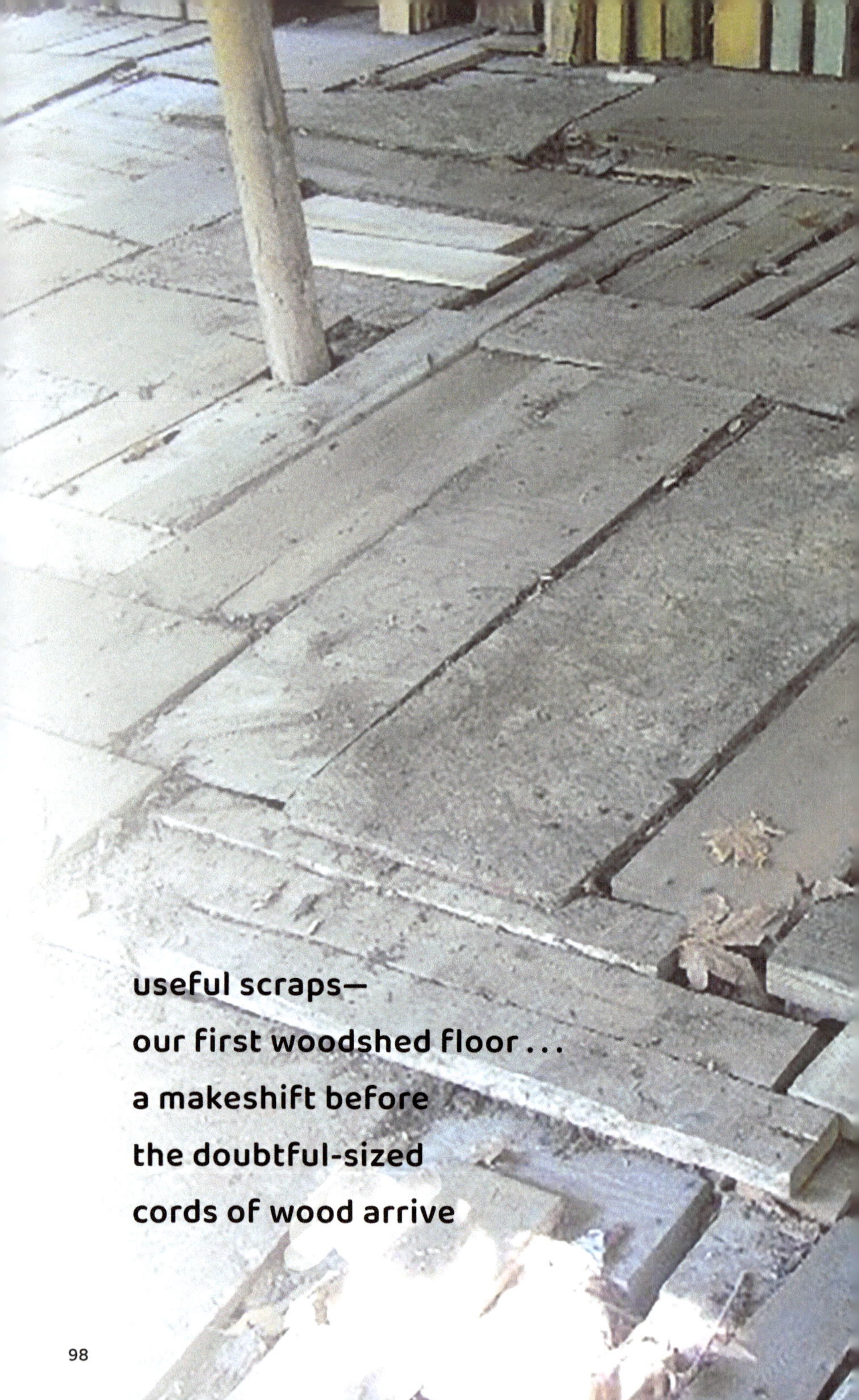

useful scraps—
our first woodshed floor . . .
a makeshift before
the doubtful-sized
cords of wood arrive

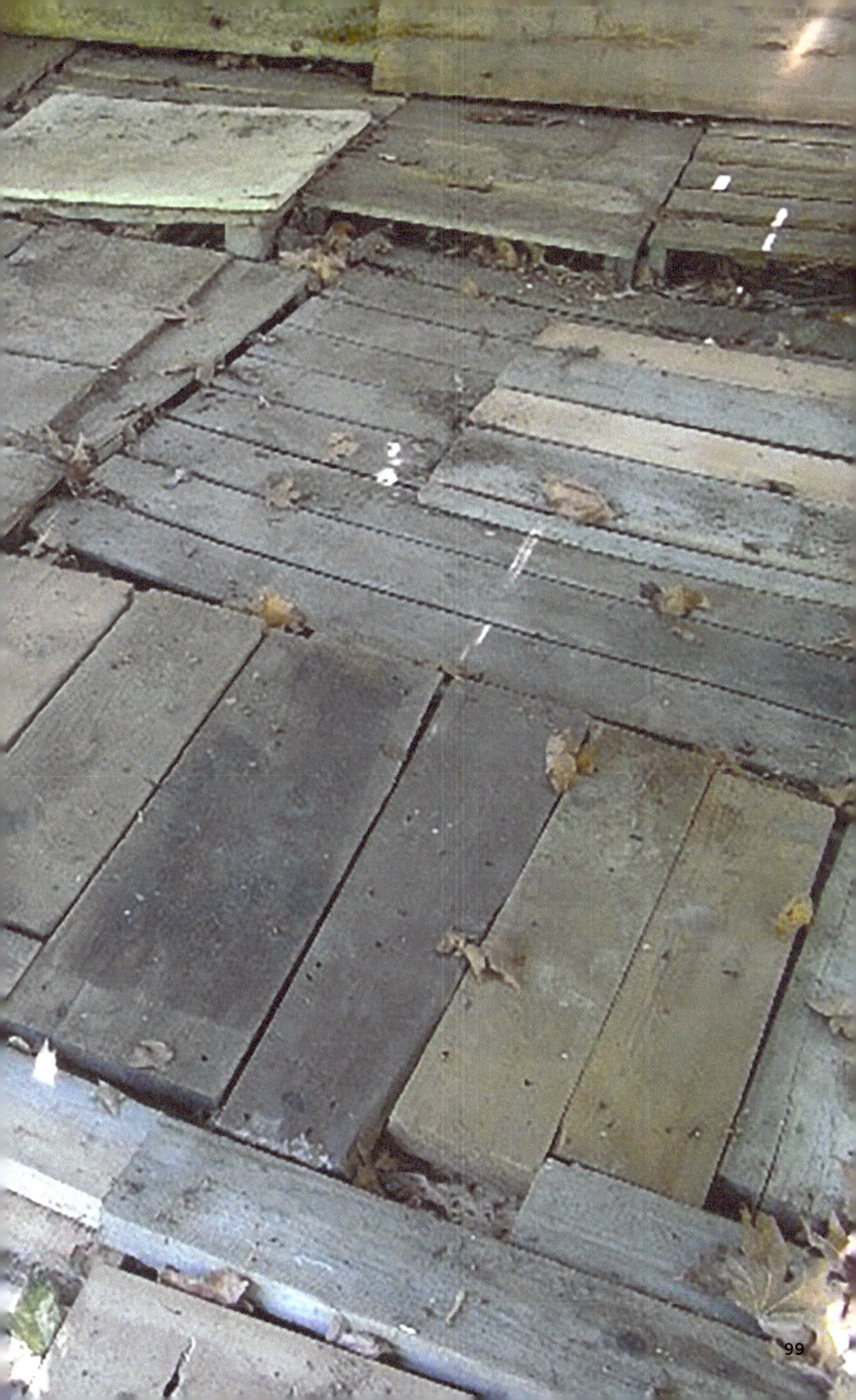

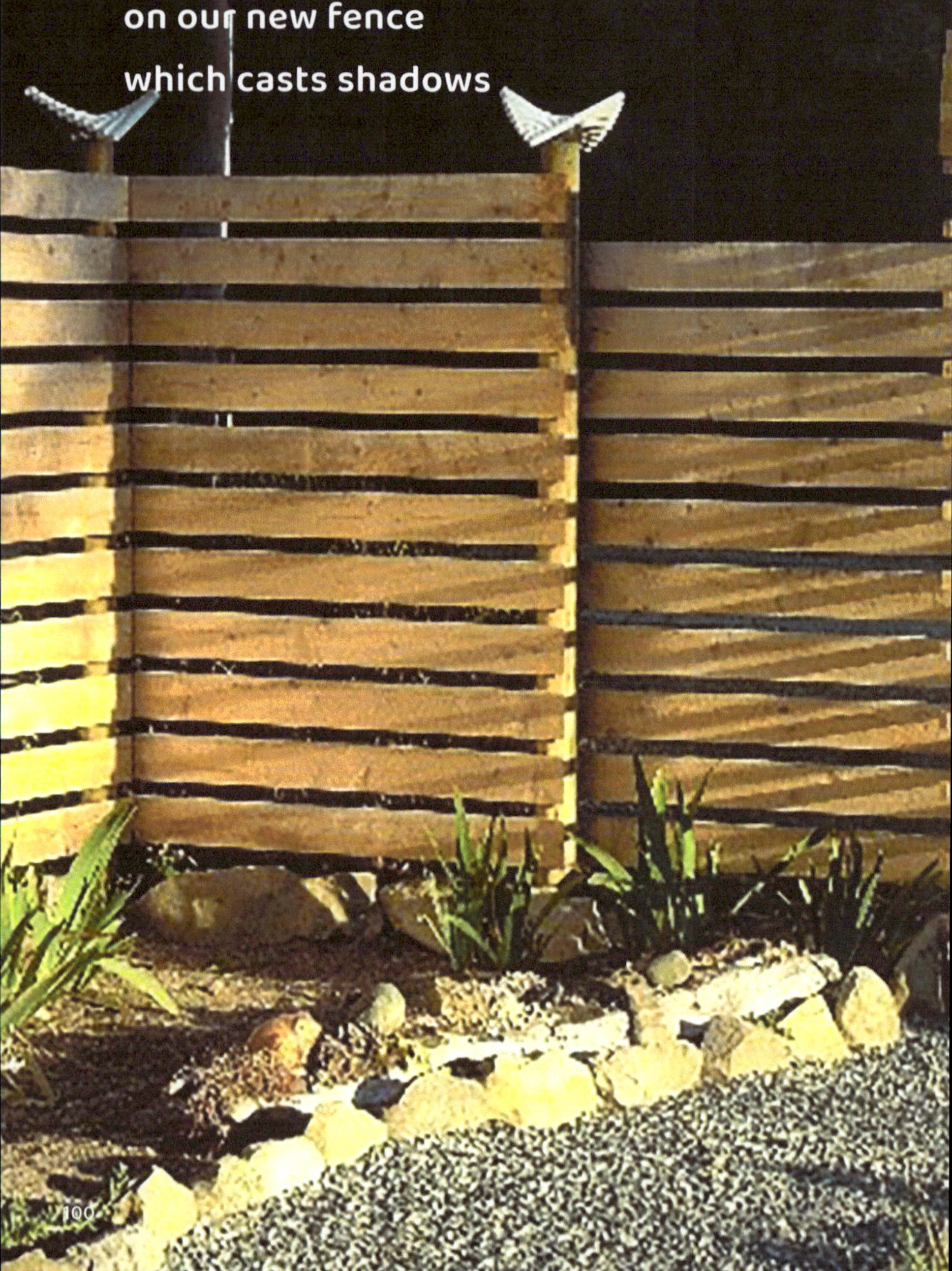

on our new fence
which casts shadows

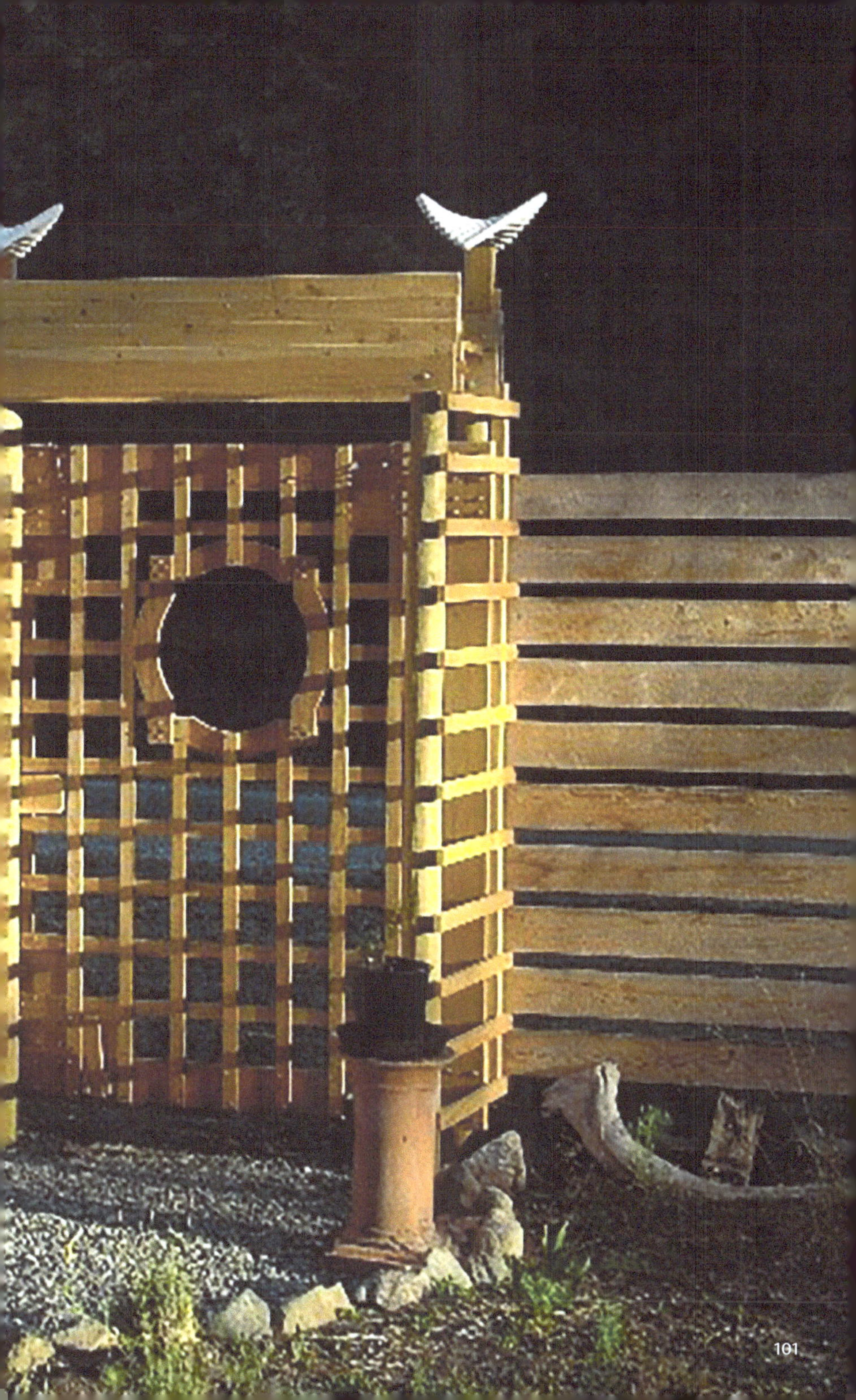

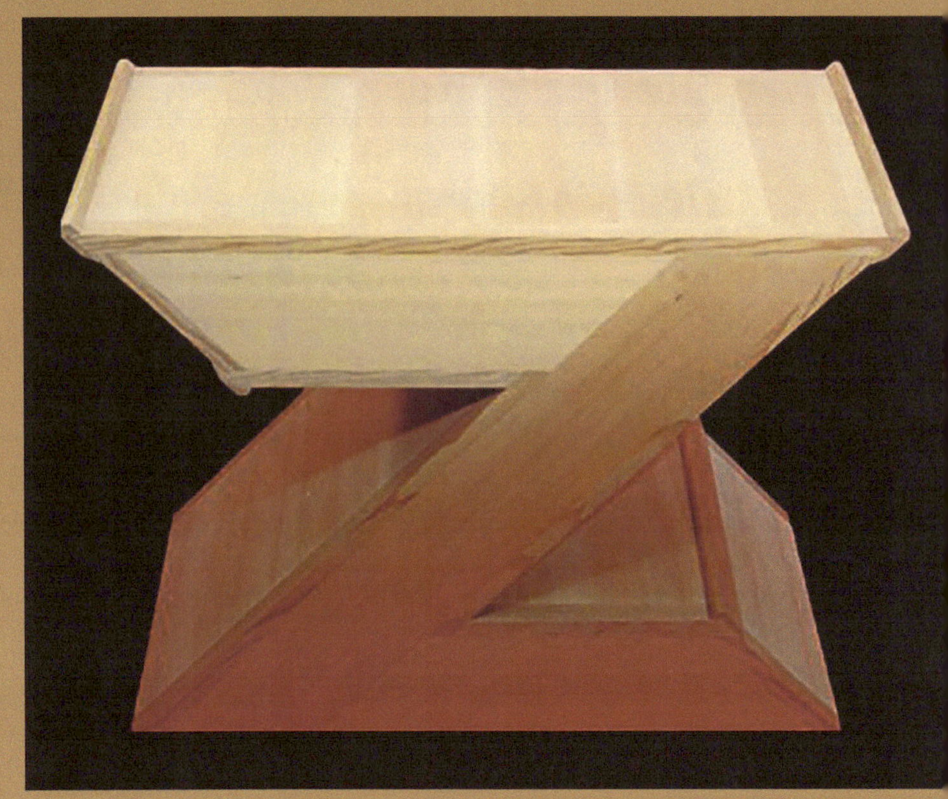

Z-Table
an obvious name
for a surprising
piece of furniture . . .
where is it now, I wonder?

this wooden cube
chose one fine spring day
to sprout forth
a great display of dried flowers
and last year's seed pods

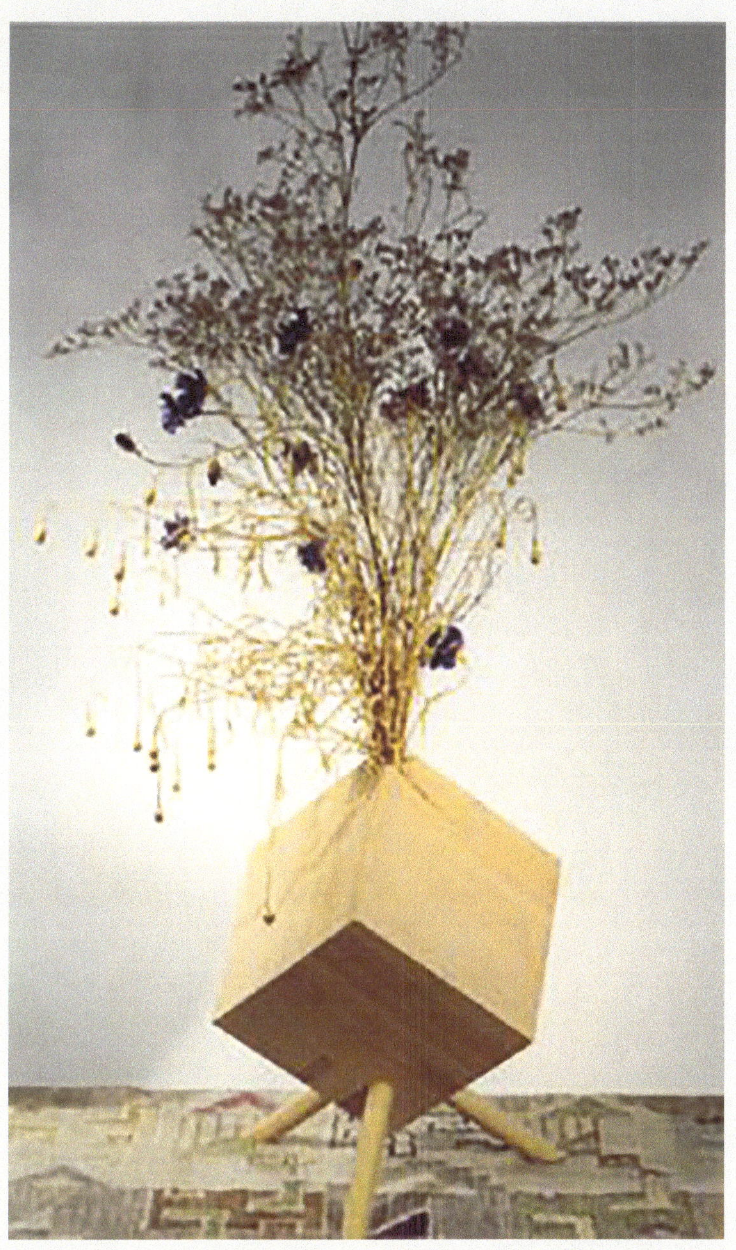

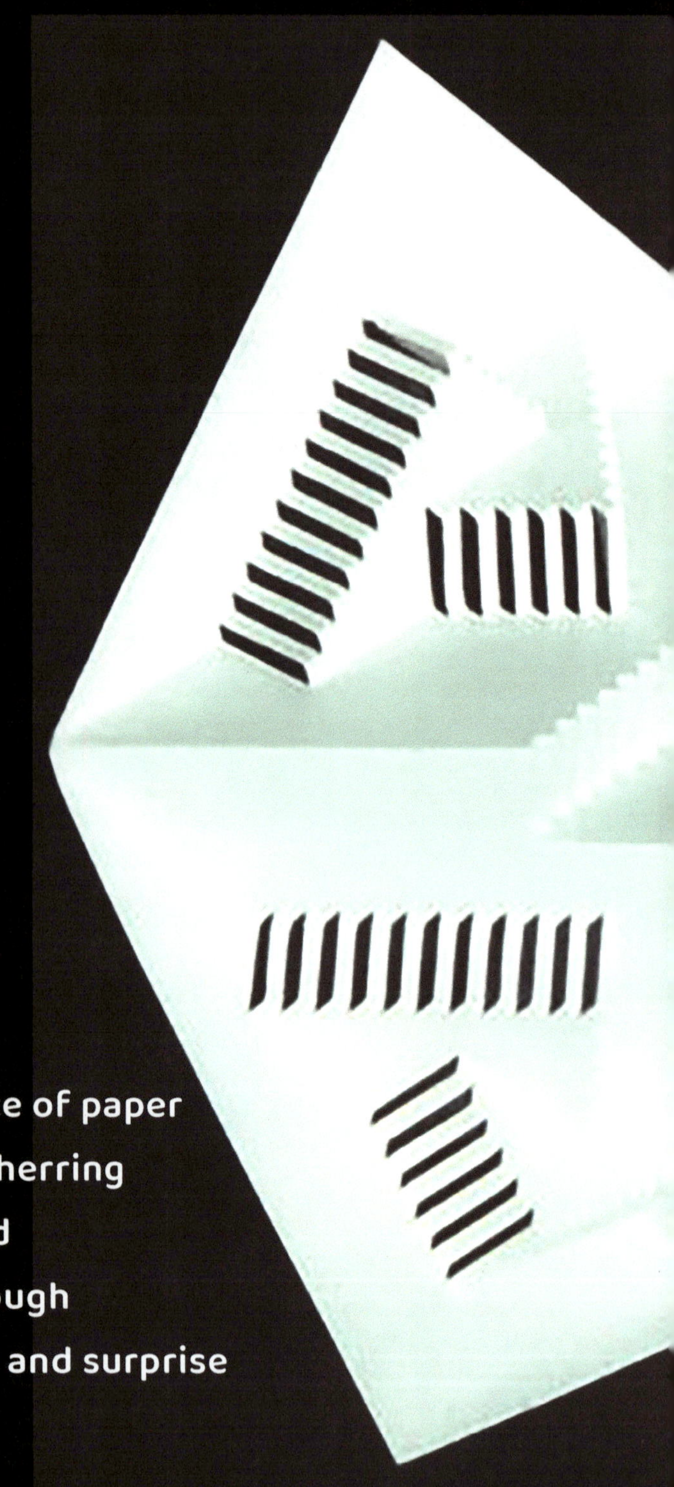

a small piece of paper
can wrap a herring
or be folded
and cut enough
to bewilder and surprise

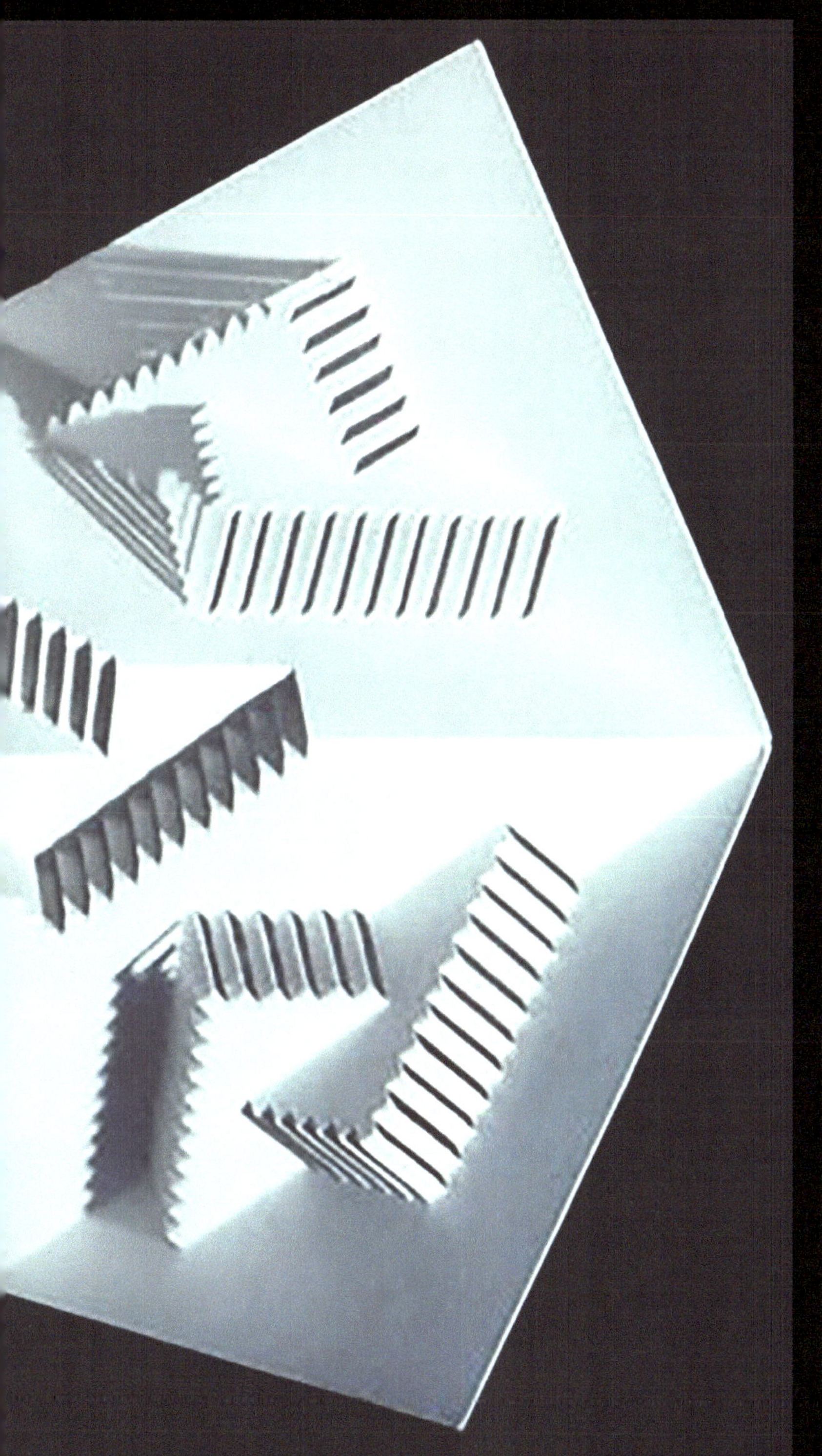

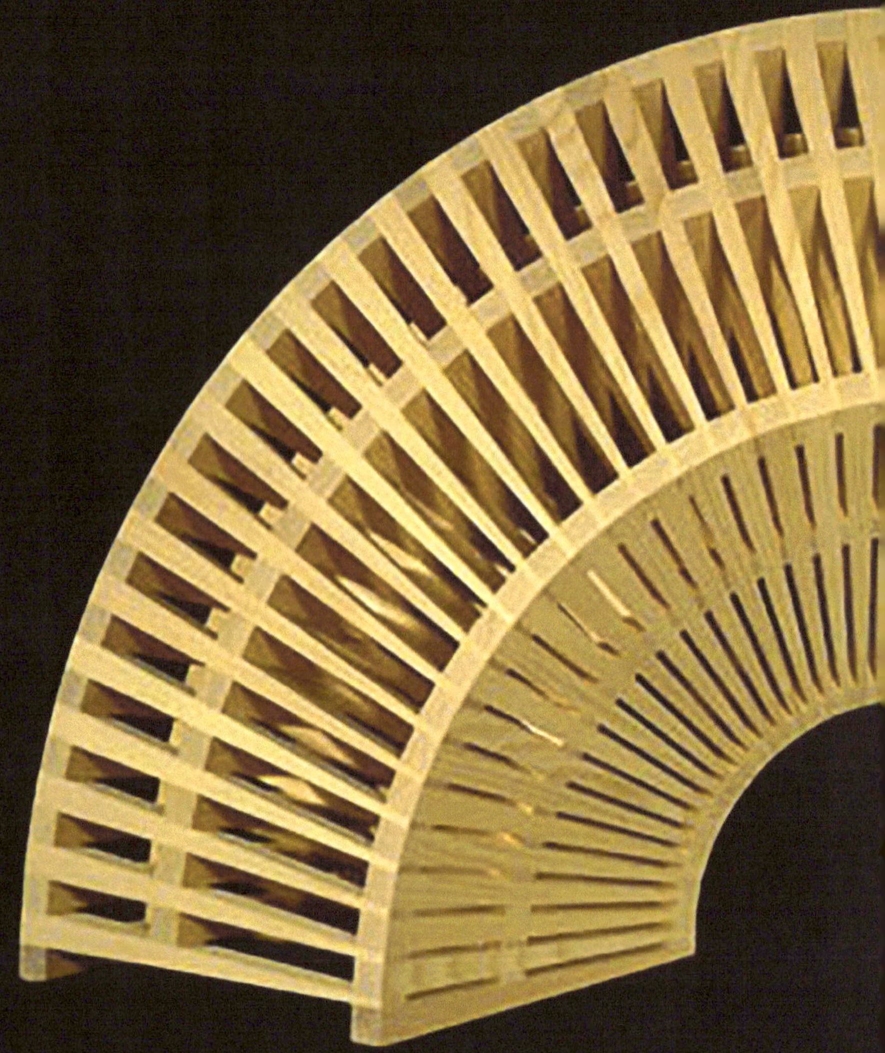

a link

a continuation

a segue

a shift from here to there

from then to now

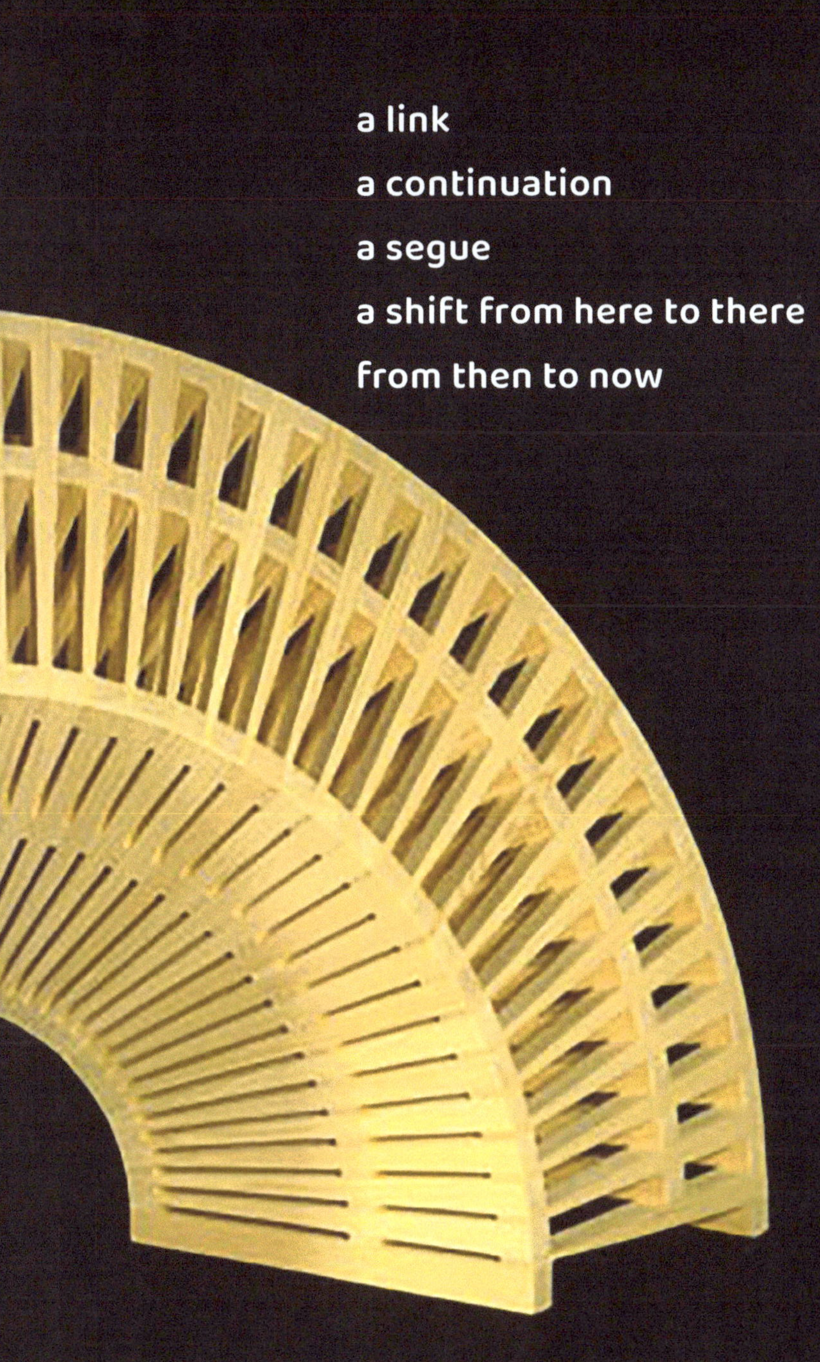

one does not write
because the goldfish play
at the bottom of the waterfall,
but because not everyone
can see them.

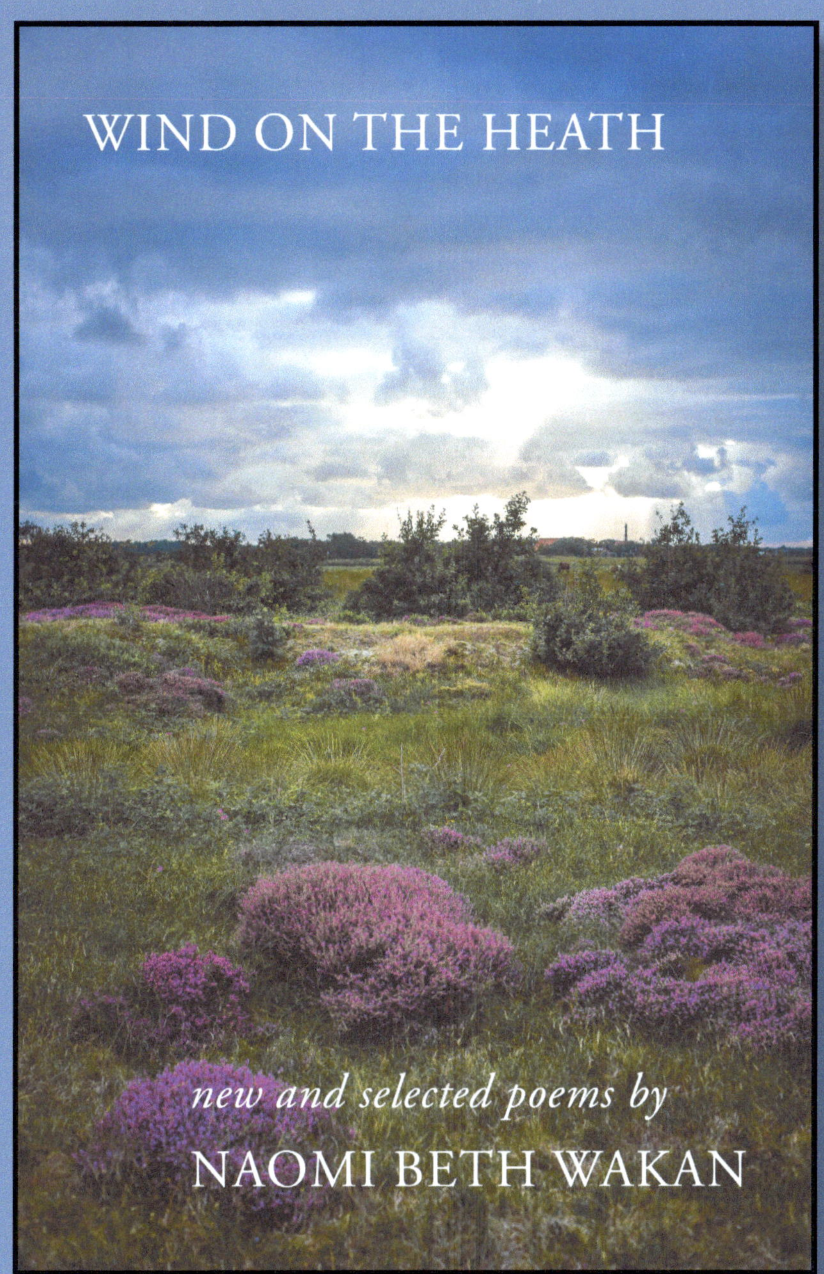
WIND ON THE HEATH
new and selected poems by
NAOMI BETH WAKAN

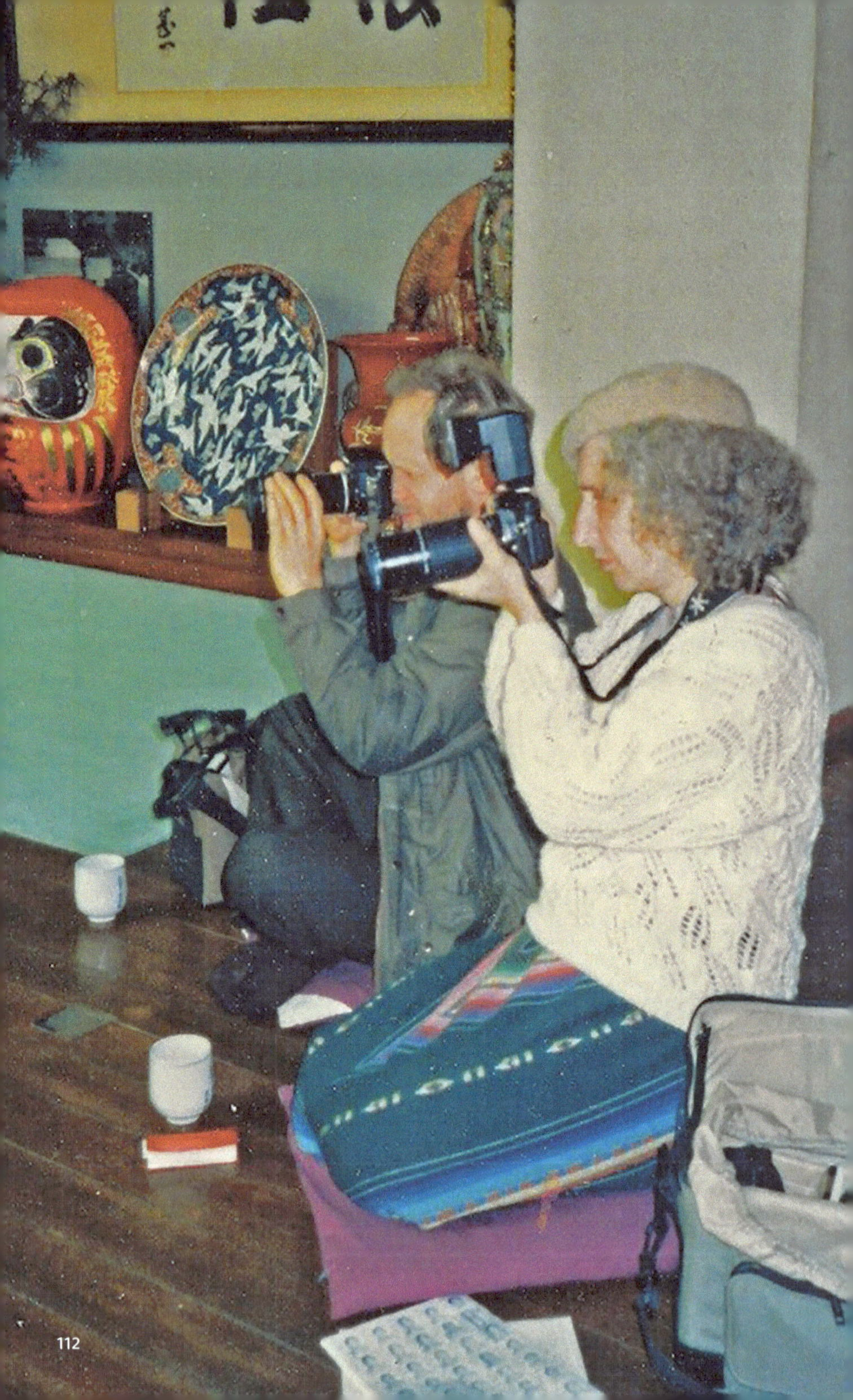

two artists
under one roof . . .
not a thing
that folks recommend,
yet here we are

Photography Notes

(all photos are © Elias Wakan unless otherwise noted; numbers below refer to page numbers)

10/11	Condensation
12/13	Bearded Iris from the Wakans' garden
14/15	Poppy from the Wakans' garden
16/17	Frost on a skylight
18/19	The Tunnel, Gabriola
20/21	Condensation
22/23	The Wakans' giant Japanese Shiro plum tree
24/25	Reflection
26/27	Tidepool, Drumbeg Park
28/29	Two of the Wakans' six gates
30/31	Otters, Drumbeg Park
32/33	The Wakans' grape vine
34/35	Garry Oak tree bark
36/37	Pears from the Wakans' orchard
38/39	Foxgloves from the Wakans' garden
40/41	Gray's Farm, Gabriola
42/43	Fall Fair, Gabriola
44/45	Elias kissing Naomi at her 80th birthday party (photo by Beverly Deutsch)
46/47	Moon seen from Gabriola Island
48/49	Japanese tea ceremony bowl
50/51	Old cabin, Gabriola

52/53	Roof tiles, Kyoto, Japan
54/55	A raspberry pick at the Wakans' home
56/57	*The Quinsam*, the old ferry from Gabriola to Nanaimo, British Columbia
58/59	Gabriola Fall Fair, The Commons
60/61	Friends at Naomi Beth Wakan's 80th birthday party
62/63	Elias Wakan swimming in winter at Drumbeg Park, Gabriola (photo by Naomi)
64/65	Iris and its shadow against the Wakans' fence
66/67	Flower petals
68/69	Girl in historical costume, Jidai Matsuri, Kyoto, Japan
70/71	The clinic Gabriolans built themselves to draw doctors to the island
72/73	Naomi reading at Nanaimo North Public Library
74/75	*Bridge joint*, Kobe, Japan
76/77	*Triumph,* made by Elias, now in a collection in the United Kingdom
78/79	Appetizers such as Naomi made for pre-Covid dinners
80/81	*Triumph* (see above)
82/83	*Release*, paint cracks on a Porsche car
84/85	*Corner Cadenza* made by Elias
86/87	Drainage pipes seen on the way to Tofino
88/89	Naomi's knitting

90/91	*Into the Void*, quilting by Naomi
92/93	Haiku gathering with Michael Dylan Welch at the Wakans' home
94/95	*Gipsy*, quilt by Naomi
96/97	Elias working on *Big Data*
98/99	First woodshed floor before it was filled with cords of wood
100/101	The Wakans' fence and gate made by Elias with wood from their property
102/103	*Z-Table*, made by Elias
104/105	*Cube Tripod*, made by Elias
106/107	*Escher Fold*, made by Elias
108/109	*Segue*, made by Elias
110/111	*Wind on the Heath, Naomi's* book covering 60 years of Naomi's poetry writing (Shanti Arts)
112/113	Elias and Naomi photographing at Sadogatake Sumo Beya, Kyoto, (photographer unknown)
119	[top] Naomi; [bottom] Elias (photo by Naomi)

Biographies

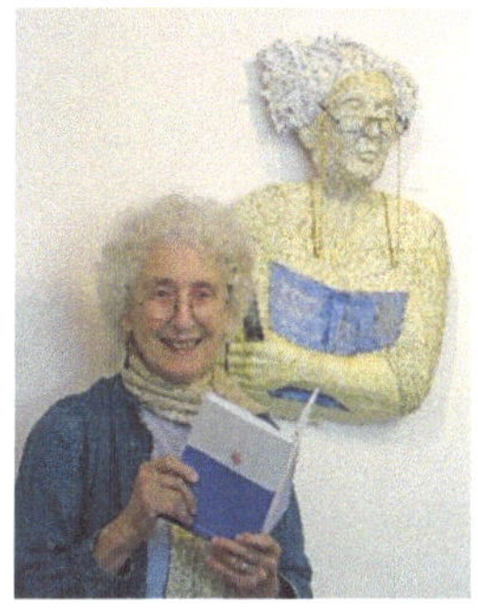

Naomi Beth Wakan is the Inaugural Poet Laureate of Nanaimo (2014–2016) and the Federation of British Columbia Writers' Inaugural Honorary Ambassador. She has published over 50 books. Her trilogy, *The Way of Tanka, The Way of Haiku,* and *Poetry That Heals* was published by Shanti Arts in 2019. Naomi is a member of The League of Canadian Poets, Haiku Canada, and Tanka Canada. She lives on Gabriola Island, British Columbia, with her husband, the sculptor Elias Wakan.
—www.naomiwakan.com

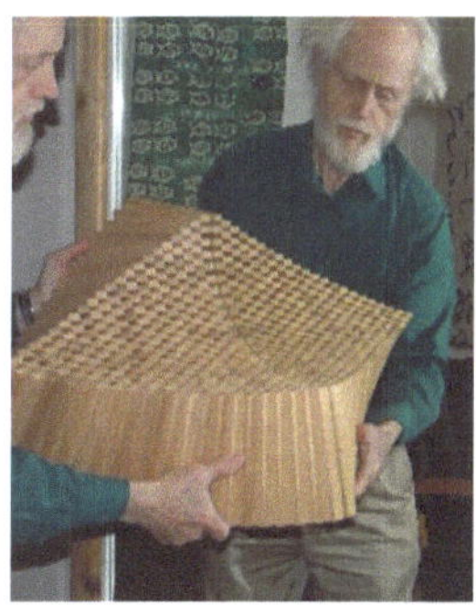

Elias Wakan studied mathematics and philosophy at Stanford University. Later, he became interested in algorithmic constructivism as an art form, and as soon as his studio and workshop were established on Gabriola, his paper maquettes began to be translated into constructions using multiple identical wood units. His works are in collections across Canada and abroad. Two of his pieces were chosen by the Canadian government to go in diplomatic offices abroad. See his complete portfolio:
—www.eliaswakan.com

www.ingramcontent.com/pod-product-compliance
Lightning Source LLC
LaVergne TN
LVHW052305100826
845147LV00006B/678

* 9 7 8 1 9 5 6 0 5 6 4 1 9 *